seasons of my garden

seasons
of
my
garden

by marjorie harris
photography by andreas trauttmansdorff

HarperCollins *Publishers Ltd*

Cypripedium reginae, showy lady's slipper

SEASONS OF MY GARDEN
Copyright © 1999 by Marjorie Harris.

For information address HarperCollins Publishers Ltd,
55 Avenue Road, Suite 2900,
Toronto, Ontario, Canada M5R 3L2.

http://www.harpercanada.com

HarperCollins books may be purchased for educational, business, or sales
promotional use. For information please write: Special Markets Department,
HarperCollins Canada, 55 Avenue Road, Suite 2900, Toronto, Ontario,
Canada M5R 3L2.

First HarperCollins hardcover ed. ISBN 0-00-255755-X
First HarperCollins trade paper ed. ISBN 0-00-638504-4

Book design by Alice Unger

Canadian Cataloguing in Publication Data

Harris, Marjorie
Seasons of my garden

Includes index.
ISBN 0-00-255755-5

1. Gardening – Ontario – Toronto. 2. Gardens – Ontario – Toronto.
3. Harris, Marjorie – Homes and haunts – Ontario – Toronto. 4. Seasons. I. Title.
SB451.36.C3H37 1999   635'.092   C99-931014-3

99 00 01 02 03 04 Proost 6 5 4 3 2 1
Printed and bound in Belgium

To the children of the garden:
Jennifer, Chris, Sarah, Brad
and the new generation:
Nicky, Dashiel and Madeleine

For Jack, forever
MH

To Lynn
AT

contents

I garden in a climate considered to have nine months of winter. This is an exaggeration, of course. It's only five months long. Only five months, at the very least, when there's not much you can do in the way of gardening. Some people think this is an offence of nature. Get out of town, they say; find a place where it's possible to go to it all year round. But not me. I like the idea of being gardened out. And like many of the plants I've placed incorrectly in this small paradise, I've acclimatized to what I've got around me.

It took a long time to get here. We bought our house in Toronto in 1967, a first home for our new, blended family of four kids and one cat. When I looked into the backyard, I thought: "How can any one person look after all this space?" I'd never had a garden before, and the size, 19 feet wide by 100 feet deep, was fence to fence to fence of neglect and weeds.

I spent a lot of time looking at this yard while cooking, eating and even doing dishes because the back end of the house is all glass. The yard is the view. And I called it a yard because, in those days, it looked like an illustration for urban poverty. Piles of construction muck, broken glass and things flung out of a house being torn to pieces. The weeds were so tall, I remember my son Chris falling asleep amidst them in the hot sunshine, and we had the devil's own time trying to find him. It was a good place for flashlight tag in those days. Great for forts and fantasies.

It was awful that first winter. The fences sagged. Nothing seemed to have grown, and what remained were bent-over thistles and other unidentified things that I was sure were bad. There were no shrubs, a dying maple and, just peeping over the fence next door, a cute little weeping willow that the neighbors had planted a year or so earlier. At least the weeping willow looks good, I thought.

A real clean-up began the following spring, but removing all the garbage took most of the summer. It wasn't until that autumn that I could actually see what we had. The garden, as such, seemed to be two narrow bands of earth along the edge of fences that ran east to west, and a long strip of very ratty-looking grass. It emphasized the bowling-alley aspect of the yard. And, if there was to be any more of a garden, I was going to have to work around the antics of four lively kids. It was decided, but not by me, that the back third of the garden would have a basketball hoop complete with tarmac to play on. I wanted a deck back there, which I pretentiously referred to as my Moon-Viewing Platform but which was really a way to keep my eye on kids playing ball, making forts or building sandboxes of varying size and complexity.

When I started out, I concentrated on the sunny spot near the house, where we'd built another deck for what turned into family living. The kids more or less ruled the rest of the place. I planted vegetables because that's what my parents had done, and I remembered how to put string down to make the rows, put boards in between rows so as not to compact the soil and to water regularly. We ate what I grew with pleasure. The raccoons got the corn, though we had a lot of fun working out ways to discourage them.

But things catch up with you in nature, and outside forces make radical changes on even the most wary of persons. What changed my life was the year the vegetables just didn't seem to want to grow. It was my first major lesson in how important observation is to gardening. That "cute" little weeping willow had grown to such a size that I now had a shady garden with patches of sun. How could it have turned into a monster without my noticing it? Don't we really look around us in the city and see what's there?

Apparently not in my case. This surprised me because I think of myself as a child of nature, someone who grew up preferring to be in the woods rather than out on the streets of whatever town we lived in. My major childhood memories are of being in Labrador, collecting leaves, collating information on wildflowers and tearing about scaring myself half to death if I actually saw a wild animal on the trail (bear once, moose once, foxes many times).

Living in the city had somehow made me lose my sensitivity to nature, and it was shocking. But I did realize that I must allow the garden to become my teacher. That I must learn much more about it. For instance, if I couldn't grow vegetables, I would grow flowers. And if it was to be flowers, let them be lovely old-fashioned ones such as daisies and marguerites. Innocently, my first move was to fill the narrow borders with perennials carefully placed at a distance from each other with lots of impatiens and petunias to add splashes of color.

I planted perennials because it seemed cheaper to have something come up every year: hardy primroses, chives, English daisies (*Bellis perennis*), peony, cushion mum, bellflower (*Campanula*, though no designation), alpine blue aster, lambs' ears, delphinium, pinks (*Dianthus*), lavender, yarrow, old roses, coneflower, campion (*Lychnis*), irises, red hot poker. And I discovered lilies: *Lilium* 'Scarlet Emperor' and 'Dragon's Blood' and *L.* x *testaceum*.

I had instinctively chosen, no doubt because they were so readily available, such traditional shrubs as purple-leaf sand cherry, weeping mulberry, red-twig dogwood and a serviceberry because I liked the bark. If anyone had told me at the time that these were really good, hardy plants, I'd have stared blankly.

The *pièce de résistance* was a Japanese maple called *Acer palmatum* 'Dissectum Atropurpureum'. This turned into one of my best investments, although, naturally, I didn't know it then. It was expensive ($19) and graceful, with a low, fountain-like form, and I could gaze at it to my heart's content in all four seasons. Of course, it was tightly corseted by grass, which was about the same as putting it in green concrete. Voilà, without even knowing it, I had made the perfect North American garden of the 1970s. And so it stayed, except for the addition of some shrubs, judicious pruning of the dying maple, cleaning out the willow debris and planting more perennials in the daisy family.

The garden survived my lack of knowledge. What I slowly discovered (lots of digging) were the deposits left during ancient ice ages. The endless motion of the incredibly deep Lake Iroquois smoothed out the glacial till that comprised its bottom, filling it with sands and clay. It formed a shoreline from 50 to 75 feet high that I can still see as a distant hill as I wander through the garden. It is always there to remind me that nothing stays the same in nature.

When the lake receded 10,000 years ago, it left a plane sloping toward our Lake Ontario. And one of the most important manifestations of this giant geological move was Taddle Creek, which carved out some of the picturesque and deep ravines that are the hallmark of this city. Taddle Creek ran through our property. And as soon as the area was populated in the 18th century, it was used as a sewage dump. Many of the ravines were filled for sewers. The touch of man is never benign.

In the second half of the 19th century, the area was subdivided into farms. Our lot was once part of a fruit farm, and in early spring when the trees are in bloom, it's possible to get a sense of this century-old imprint. These farms were subdivided and then subdivided again as the town encroached on the country. Our lot is a deep one by city standards because we were at the edge of Seaton Pond, which Taddle Creek flowed into. It was a marshy edge, and thus the houses were placed at some distance from both the marsh and the murky waters. In 1883, the area (known as The Annex) was annexed to the village of Yorkville, and our creek was funneled through cement pipes to contain the pollution.

This is a city of neighborhoods defined by the ravines. Our streets are lined with maples, silver and Norway, and there is a cooling canopy all around. Now, one can only imagine having a creek run through the bottom of the garden, and in my mind's eye, it will always be there. Its presence is certainly with us in spring. Each year, the groundwater rises and floods the garden. It was not always thus. Behind us, we once had a huge garden filled with trees and shrubs. Everything was chopped down to make way for a parking lot. Ergo, the flood. No amount of hydrological activity on my part can avert this. It happens.

At the garden's urging, I became an observer, filling notebooks with the daily weather, the plants in bloom and what I should be doing given the givens. The winds around Toronto come from the west, and it's typical here that stormy, wet periods are followed by dry, settled conditions. We receive about 31 inches of rain annually, fairly evenly distributed throughout the year, except between the middle of July and the end of September, when it's pretty dry.

We suffer temperature extremes that drive most Torontonians crazy. The lake water off the city is very cool, but it does modify some of the arctic outbreaks that plague areas farther to the north and east. We get mild flows of southwesterly winds in winter followed by frigid northwest circulation. Our freeze–thaw cycles and drastic temperature changes make cautious gardeners of us all.

By the mid-1980s, I could feel myself becoming more and more drawn by the garden. I found a book by Russell Page, *The Education of a Gardener*, which promptly turned things around. I could not only read about gardening, I enjoyed it.

But what happened in 1986 was a turning point. I was sitting drinking coffee one morning, staring out into a soft fall of snow, musing in the kind of pearly winter light that flattens everything. What a totally dull bit of ground out there, I remember thinking. I stared and stared. Creative staring, it turned out, because before long I could *see* what it should look like. What appeared in my vision was that the first third should have a checkerboard of stones and it should be crammed with plants. What I saw out there was a jungle, a massing of plants quite unlike anything I was aware of seeing before. I didn't care about what happened to the rest of the garden. It was this one section that haunted me. I still have the little notebooks where I attempted to work out what size the stones would be, how far apart, how many, the width and depth. Over and over and over, these drawings crop up in my junk (journalists never throw anything out).

I had no idea of how to go about doing any of this, which by now had me on fire. I ordered up the 2-by-2-foot patio stones, and as they were dumped on the front lawn (well, sort of lawn), I realized I hadn't made a plan for getting them to the back or putting them in place. Family and friends tried lifting them and quickly drifted away. But I was lucky. I happened to know a landscape architect who said he'd let me "have" one of his best gardeners for two days — not a minute longer, since this was the beginning of the busy season. It turned out to be two of the best, most useful days of my life.

When the gardener turned up, I asked him to scrunch his eyes and envision this place in three or five years with the checkerboard filled in and the place dense with plants. He knew exactly what I meant and proposed lifting all the grass and making a berm in the center.

A berm? I didn't even know the word, let alone that it's a rise at least 4 feet high and more than 10 feet long. It will give the place some contour, he said. Well, I could certainly envision that. As he pulled up each square of turf, he knocked off the soil, turned it upside down and started sculpting the berm in the center section of the garden. A brilliant stroke, and he got it just right. Each time I walk by it, I bless his insight. A boring, flat space becomes animated.

The scale of a half-moon 20 feet long and 10 feet at its widest fit in with the garden perfectly. A path would skirt it and add sorely needed mystery. If he'd been the slightest bit off, there would have been almost no way of correcting it, since the volume of soil would have been impossible to move. This made a natural room out of the center section of the garden. I covered the hump with manure and compost and planted a groundcover called creeping Jenny, *Lysimachia nummularia*, which would serve to hold back any erosion until the rest of the plants caught up.

I also realized, standing on the deck that day looking at the yard so naked without any grass, that this is what a blank canvas must be all about. "This is where I can make my imprint." I was somewhat intimidated by the thought. Even though a gardener is not, after all, setting out to make a work of Art, it seemed extravagant to say, "I will now make a garden." What gardens I knew were in books, and they all seemed impossibly lavish, far beyond my cramped space and limited

means. What I wanted was a place that would satisfy me esthetically and give me something I could handle alone. It seemed an enormous challenge at the time, especially when I looked at all the empty spaces between the stones and the hugely barren berm.

I knew enough to know that I'd better get cracking if I was going to build a garden that would succeed. I read what books I could find, and they were few at the time, about perennials, about design (the classic book on the subject, *Garden Design,* by Sylvia Crowe), but most importantly, about soil. I had good soil. I knew just by its feel in my hands (crumbly, friable) and the smell (absolutely pure and, well, earthy). By then, I'd learned a lot about my land and knew that it was on the clayey side, which was good from a nutritional point of view, bad if I wanted to grow ericaceous plants. Which naturally I did because I probably couldn't.

It was very much the trend in the 1980s to have rhododendrons in our city. How or why, I don't know, since most of the soil is either heavy clay or very sandy. But we all wanted them, nurseries were selling them, and in winter, most gardens looked like horrendous bundles of mummies with shrubs muffled against the howling winds. I didn't want that, but I was told they'd acclimatize after four years or so.

So I dutifully planted *Rhododendron catawbiense* 'Nova Zembla', *Kalmia latifolia* 'Shooting Star' and *Pieris japonica* 'Mountain Fire'. All good plants and all completely inappropriate for my little woodland with its rich, very unacidic soil. I dug in peat moss, friends gave me pine needles, and I watched these plants struggle and never flourish. I still have them 15 years later and they still struggle, but they are surrounded by plants that do love it here.

It was a major lesson. To be a good gardener is to grow plants really well, and that means finding the right plant for its place. This is so much more important than whatever trendy thing is coming down the pike. I had already planted sensible things years before: the serviceberry, *Amelanchier canadensis* (my favorite plant to this day), and a dogwood with red bark, both now more than 30 years old. The weeping mulberry having outlived its usefulness — too big, too gnarled — was removed by my protesting son. It was the tree of his childhood. But it's important not to sentimentalize plants.

What I had in mind originally was an English cottage garden much as I'd seen in books, a garden filled with herbaceous plants that disappear all winter. I slowly realized, however, that given our long cold season, this would look pretty dreary. What worked well was right in front of me: the shrubs I'd planted. Unlike herbaceous perennials, woody plants are with us year-round. They have definition during the winter, they hold snow, many have bark that improves in the cold, and some even hang onto their leaves in spite of winter. These revelations certainly changed the way I wanted to garden.

I learned to make a mixed border with a few annuals, lots of perennials and, as the years went by, increasing numbers of woody plants. What I wanted was more a tapestry than a painting. Something subtle, with various elements artfully interwoven. The longer I garden and the older I get, the more I favor woody plants for their endurance and flexibility.

This has been another slow route. My eye was trained by looking at paintings during the many years I'd worked in an art gallery. When I started, I wanted great splashes of color and plenty of them. This is all very fine but splashes don't last for long. As my tastes have changed, so have my plants. What endures are the shrubs and trees, and what gets moved out usually are the perennials. I don't have room for huge drifts of color. I add it as an accent rather than as the main attention-getter.

Now, I'm looking more for ambiance and lushness than a strict design. Foliage color can provide a theme as well as add texture to a garden. What I didn't have was some kind of design in mind for shrubs and small trees and soon discovered to my dismay that you can't just be hauling them in and out of the ground all the time. Woody plants will have a good two-year sulk after a big move; a perennial will look good the next season.

Eventually, I saw layer after layer of color and texture so that the eye would immediately have the sense of many plants and then be drawn beyond to a few major plants and then on to another undulation of color and texture, and so on through the whole garden. It would be impossible to see all the garden at once, but it would present a vibrant and sensual picture when viewed as a whole.

Large shrubs throughout, very often at the front of a border, bestow a lively amount of choreography. I put in as many perennials as I can to complement them on all sides, always making an attractive profile for each plant from every point of view. The most successful important plants are two near the deck: the red-leafed rose, *Rosa glauca* (syn. *R. rubrifolia*), which looks so lovely in winter with huge, orangey-red hips. It is balanced on the other side of the garden by the coralbark maple, *Acer palmatum* 'Sango-kaku'. This is a sensational plant with an elongated vase shape. In spring, it has pale yellow leaves that become more intense as the season draws along. In winter, the colder the weather, the more vivid the red bark. The two plants make an almost natural arch as they lean toward each other.

The way I like to garden is in sections or rooms, it doesn't matter what you call them. And then go from that macrocosm down to the microcosms of small pockets in each section. This way, there are fewer disappointments, and what I'm trying to achieve in each small space gives a huge amount of pleasure. So what if it doesn't quite work all around; here is a small success I can see.

The way the garden has ended up is so close to my first image that I sometimes find it eerie. The checkerboard abuts the house and is crammed with plants flowing gently from one height to another. They make it impossible to run through this garden. It has become very much a stroll garden with stepping stones along the way, making you stop and appreciate some small scene, twist one way then another, then turn back to see where you've come from. Each time it looks different, which is exactly what we want: perpetual change. There are large, important shrubs (viburnums) and large perennials (huge eupatoriums) that prove you don't have to have bitty plants in a bitty garden. Drama sweeps its way to the center section.

This is the berm and the woodland. When any visitor moves into this section, they take a deep breath. It's somehow quieter and certainly cooler here, with a distinctive feeling of its own — dappled shade — contrasting with the rest of the garden. It's under the huge canopy of the weeping willow, the only tree on this earth I truly loathe.

Much in gardening is about attitude, and I have a bad one toward that willow. It's wrong for the city, and I'm scared of it. It's dangerous in a wind and drops debris all the time. So far, it hasn't taken out too many plants, but I get enough snapped tops to keep my dander up. I long for its death and the possibility of putting in really good city plants that will be habitat for birds and animals.

And yet, and yet, it makes a stunning background to my plants, which is something I recognized all those years ago. I started looking after it, and I learned to garden in spite of this giant.

I dubbed the back third of my garden Le Jardin des Refusés because it was the place where I put all the plants I couldn't figure out what to do with. Once the basketball tarmac was removed, it took three years to revive the soil, and I put my leftovers in this space. Over time, this rather lazy feature became more and more organized. There is now a bench on a small, semicircular stone terrace. The rest of the area has been divided into a quadrangle by old bricks. I try things out here: new plants as well as planting patterns and combinations. The area, however, has settled in with its own look, and I'm very pleased with it most days.

The work of the garden goes on throughout the year. I make lists all winter long, ignore them usually, and just get out and do what each season allows me to do. I am almost never frustrated by my garden. If it has taught me one thing, it's to be patient except for that late-winter speeding-up of the heart when I am finally convinced spring will come again.

Left: This is what I started with: enough grass to give the yard that green concrete bowling alley look, tight little perennial borders and out-of-place tchotchkes (the lady and the fishing ball). The *Acer palmatum* was further back, waiting for its new home. Below: This was taken about two minutes after the gardener finished installation of the checkerboard. He created a berm perfectly in scale in the centre room. Beyond that is the moon-viewing platform. It was ripped out a few years later to make way for the Jardin des Refusés. This also started the habit of taking pictures of the garden every few weeks.

must-have books

• *A-Z Encyclopedia of Garden Plants*, Christopher Brickell, Trevor Cole and Judith D. Zuk, Editors-in-Chief. Montreal: Reader's Digest Association (Canada) Ltd., 1997.
• *Adventures With Hardy Bulbs*, by Louise Beebe Wilder. New York: The Lyons Press, 1998 (reprint of her 1936 classic).
• *The Best of the Hardiest*, by John J. Sabuco. Flossmoor, Illinois: Plantmen's Publications, 3rd edition, 1990.
• *The Education of a Gardener*, by Russell Page. London: Harvill Press, 1994 (reprint of the 1962 classic published by William Collins Son & Co.).
• *Garden Design*, by Sylvia Crowe. London: Sotheby's Publications, 3rd edition, 1994 (reprint of her 1959 classic).
• *Manual of Woody Landscape Plants: Their Identification, Ornamental Characteristics, Culture, Propagation and Use*, by Michael A. Dirr. Champaign, Illinois: Stipes Publishing Co., 5th edition, 1998.

spring

There may be life before gardening, but what other life is there once a garden possesses your soul?

After evolving into an obsessive gardener, I find it impossible to imagine living without a garden. The intensity of this feeling overwhelms me every spring. How did I exist before this? The answer lies in the pure beauty of its presence. There is the scent to drive one mad with pleasure. I love the smell of the earth newly released from its blanket of snow and mulch. I am astonished at these marvelous things that rise tumescent from the black soil. Every year, I am in awe of their power to captivate my imagination.

No matter what winter dishes up or how many months it lasts, there is a sense of hope and longing. Hope that the garden has made it through another major siege, and longing to see something, anything, that speaks of spring renewal. If the garden survives, then so will I, says the gardener. The garden is, of course, filled with life even when nothing is particularly obvious. What we really need, however, is a sign of something shouting a hallelujah for endurance.

This could happen when the delicate blossoms of a witch hazel dangle from its branches like butterflies at rest. But this comes in February — much too soon. This is a false promise. No, spring's sweetest moment is the first tip of a bulb barely visible above the snow. Then we know a new season will emerge even when it feels as though these grim and gray days will never go away. Winter aconite's tiny splotches of gold, *Iris reticulata*'s brave cobalt blue, snowdrops and crocus nodding valiantly in bitter winds. It's a sight to melt the hardest heart.

These bulbs, like so many plants here, were carelessly tossed about, placed without a moment's thought to their future in the easiest spot I could find. They've rewarded me by multiplying and running about in areas where I can see them from every window in the house. Each year, they serve as a reminder that much in gardening is serendipitous. So many of these perfectly placed groups were sheer accident. The gardening ego, however, doesn't mind accepting compliments for such cleverness in thinking up this or that bit of brilliance.

Spring arrives late here. All through March, temperatures are low, and freezing nights persist although the snow melts and plants elbow past last year's detritus. Cool, damp air blows off the lake, and though there is usually one more snowfall at the end of April, we know the final frost is early May. As far as I'm concerned, that's planting time. Our ancestors, however, divined that May 24 would be a safe date, and it's a habit that persists. It's much too late for me because the garden season seems way too short to hesitate or be cautious. The parcels from distant nurseries start arriving by May 1, earlier if I order from the West Coast. I use a set of old bedsheets to cover everything up if there's a spot of frost, but normally I don't have to bother.

This place is always a mess in spring. I let things go in the autumn for the birds that flap about here all winter long. The seeds, the vines and the leaves left untouched are for their benefit. Or so I say.

Serviceberry, *Amelanchier canadensis*, was one of my first acquisitions. It's still my favorite shrub and I think every garden should have one. It's hardy and has this glorious froth of spring flowers. They turn into deep purple berries which birds adore (the berries are edible but who ever gets a chance). In autumn, the color is a rich red. This is a view from the berm with a tapestry of pulmonarias, hostas and a great grass called *Phalaris arundinacea* 'Feesey's Form'. It's not as rampant as the common form of gardener's garters and looks good for three seasons. The other shrub is a variegated nannyberry, *Viburnum lentago* 'Variegatum'.

The dreaded spring flood is a result of having all the surrounding trees ripped out plus the rise of underground streams and now-covered pond. The upside is that this brings rich nutrients into the garden right to the lady's head. The hose leads from a dry well where a sump pump starts up when things get too bad. We run the hose out to the front street into the sewer. My neighbors say they know it's spring for sure when they see all this rigged up. I don't worry because, a few weeks later, everything is burgeoning.

Somehow it seems much more sensible to leave it all for spring, when I'm full of beans and ready for just about anything the garden has to offer. I'm all set to crawl about the earth wearing an old pair of leather gloves flipping things out of the way to catch the first glimpses of new hosta shoots and the first slug ready to munch its way through these delicate creatures. It gets my blood up to speed just collecting these monstrosities. There are few things I hate in the garden, but slugs have to top the list, and stomping is about the only truly effective way of getting rid of them.

And then there is the annual flood. In the early days, there was a triple lot behind us filled with wildflowers and an incredible array of century-old shrubs and trees, plus an owner who'd been there since birth. At her death, the whole place was razed for a parking lot. I've never felt so sick at the sound of man and machines as at that time. It took only two days to remove decades of growth.

We were stunned a year later to see the groundwater rise to smother half our yard. And it became painfully apparent that we were the lowest garden on two streets, with at least five gardens draining into ours. Gone was the intricate system of roots that had utilized the water. That first year, the kids and I tried bailing, mucking about in rubber boots and sloshing about in warm spring sunshine. We gave up when it became obvious that though this might be fun, it was hopeless. For years, the spring garden was where rafts sailed and kids got soaking wet until the ground thawed completely and could absorb the water.

When I became a serious gardener, however, the flood also became a serious problem. Plants were dying of sogginess. Many of them were lifted right out of the soil. Oh, I got (and still get) lots of advice about putting in a bog garden. Of course, this doesn't take into account that the area is dead dry in summer and that the weeping willow sucks about 27,000 gallons of water out of the soil each day.

As an annual stopgap measure, my son Chris was cashiered into digging a dry well 4 feet deep and lining it with bricks. It was an instructive look at the profile of the soil. We have a good humus level, rich topsoil and a bit of ash (from the days of dumping furnace ash in backyards), some sandy pebbles and a hardpan of clay.

Each year, we drop a sump pump in the hole, attach all the garden hoses and run them out to the sewer. This at least drains most of the water from neighboring gardens, and it keeps mine down to a natural spring dampness. One benefit is that the rise of groundwater brings lots of nutrients from the clay-rich hardpan.

The flood is also a magnet for birds flying through. Neighbors who know better than I have counted up to 80 species. One of spring's great pleasures is watching flocks of birds come and splash about in the water. The birds must retain Seaton Pond in their genetic memories.

I wade out in Wellies to see what's managed to survive and am never disappointed. The bulbs on high ground are fine, so I've learned not to plant them in spaces that will stay too long underwater. Hostas seem impervious, as do most of the shrubs: the serviceberry, summersweet (*Clethra*), viburnums and certainly the birch look pretty good. Pulmonarias and lamiums have been astonishingly healthy. The natives, such as bloodroot (*Sanguinaria*), wild ginger (*Asarum canadense*) and small Solomon's seal (*Polygonatum biflorum*), don't just survive this assault, they seem to thrive on it. Meadowsweet (*Filipendula*) and hardy geraniums are also fine, but the poor epimediums, which normally take three or four years to make a statement, however small, need about ten years to do anything under these circumstances.

As I've said before, much in gardening is about attitude, and my attitude has become one of "Hurray, room for new plants." But this did lead me to think seriously about having some kind of water in the garden. I mused about having a pond in the flood area. Then I considered the massive leaf fall and constant debris from the willow. The rear of the garden seemed a good idea, but how often do I actually sit down there? I loved the idea of a reflecting pond in front of the keystone lady in the center of the checkerboard. Then I thought of the thousands of dollars it would cost and the possibility of leaks and repairs.

As usual with this garden, the option taken is the least expensive one. I had a wonderful old wash tub bought at a junk sale and a handsome lion's head with a little hole in his mouth purchased on a whim. He was mounted on a mirror and rigged so that the water would drip out of his mouth into the tub below, with a small circulating pump to keep the water moving. I gave up using water plants when the raccoons took to hurling them about in a terrifyingly noisy way every night.

There was one problem — the sound. It drove us all crazy. My neighbors swore it was like a dripping toilet to them. We kept turning it off because it was so irritating. Wine and drips do not mix. I settled on a pleasant little fountain pump splishing water over some wonderful old rocks found up at a friend's cottage on Georgian Bay. It's just enough to mask ambient sound, and the grandchildren adore putting their hands in it and catching the light.

I would like to say that I make a map of all the bulbs I plant. But like a lot of good intentions, it never gets done. I'm always surprised by what does come up. I usually have something in mind, but that inevitably gets interfered with by squirrels. They will drag in the odd red tulip from somewhere else and stick it in any old place. Squirrels are terrible designers. Narcissus are poisonous to these animals, but they dig them up anyway, have a look and then toss them to one side as they head for something edible.

The little bulbs of spring are enchanting. They are so easy to place you can pack them in tightly among lusher plants such as hostas, around rocks, near trees and shrubs and against fences or walls. Any place, in fact, that's difficult to design a planting for. These are just a few. Clockwise from top left: Snowdrops, *Galanthus nivalis*; *Crocus* 'Snow Bunting'; the highly sensual tips of a hosta; and *Iris reticulata*.

Left: This is one of my best bulb combinations and, happily, it's in the front garden. The deep purple, almost black, tulip is called 'Queen of Night'. You can put it with just about anything and it will look good. Here, I've got it with grape hyacinths (*Muscari*) and *Narcissus* 'Thalia'. The ground-hugging, purple-foliaged plants are heucheras. The small-leafed shrub is inkberry, *Ilex glabra*, and in the background is a climbing hydrangea, *Hydrangea petiolaris*, which threatens to eat the house. Above left: *Tulipa saxatilis* amid the brilliant blue spikes of *Scilla siberica*. Above right: *Tulipa kaufmanniana* with its striped leaves and a sprinkling of scillas.

Above left: *Tulipa* 'Shakespeare' and scillas. Above right: Yellow-and-white *Tulipa tarda* mingle with the delicate white bells of fritillaria and the variegated leaves of *Kerria japonica* 'Picta'. The red tulips were brought in, unsolicited, by squirrels. For some reason, species tulips don't seem to attract their busy little paws and appetites the way other tulips do. This may be my imagination since I love working with them so much. Tuck species tulips into corners and near up-and-coming perennials. The larger plants will disguise the yellowing bulb foliage. Most of the bulbs shown here will naturalize slowly over time, which adds to their value in the garden.

Above left: The bright magenta of *Tulipa humilis* is almost impossible to combine with anything else so I let it sit in solitary splendor. Above right: *Tulipa batalinii*, the perfect species tulip. The flowers are the softest yellow fading to peach, and the narrow leaves have a definite blue tone. There are no caveats on these plants whatsoever except to buy far more than you imagine you could possibly place. I throw them on the ground and wherever they roll is where I plant them. Always leave a few to drift away as though nature had created the design. Never lump them in rows or bunch them like posies. They should look as free and easy as possible.

There is a Spring Urge to brush everything aside and let the sun shine on cold soil. Well, one does learn something about patience after gardening long enough. And now I don't get out there in a frenzy of housekeeping fever. I leave things alone, knowing that the earliest bulbs will make their way through leaf litter and mulch without any help from me. And the slightest movement of leaves is likely to break off a delicate head. I wait until the last of the big bulbs have appeared and then move off any leftover mulch and put it in the compost. This lets the sun warm up the soil, encouraging more new growth.

When I was young and green, I was particularly attracted to a small plant named star-of-Bethlehem, *Ornithogalum umbellatum*. Pretty little starry blooms. What no one told me was that they will spread and spread and spread, that 30 years later, I'd still be picking the small, bead-like bulbs out of every plant I put in the area. There are some species that don't have this rampant quality, but I didn't know that then.

They did, however, start a love for small bulbs, especially grape hyacinths (*Muscari*) and scilla. Give them to me mixed with everything — with *Anemone blanda* or species tulips such as *Tulipa tarda* and *T. turkestanica* — or massed together to make a blanket of blue on their own. And I like them especially next to common Solomon's seal, *Polygonatum multiflorum*, whose little asparagus-like heads are among the first I see. I adore the way its heart-shaped blooms hang down from the stems later on. Eventually, alas, it becomes too rambunctious and is a toughy to root out. On the other hand, this is a good sharing plant and does move easily enough to fill in any blank spots in the woodland.

The woodland is one of the most amiable parts of my garden. In spring, it's smothered in bulbs, and in winter, it is clad in the foliage of dozens of evergreen plants. The latter may look a bit sad at first, but they make up for it in the long run. The woodland in spring is a bit of heaven. Consider all the things planted in it: Virginia bluebells (*Mertensia virginica*); spring beauty (*Claytonia*); hepatica; hellebores; bloodroot (*Sanguinaria canadensis*); trilliums, white and red; *Brunnera*, plain and variegated; both native and European gingers (*Asarum* spp.); and dog's-tooth violets (*Erythronium*). Hundreds of bulbs are only a harbinger of what's to come. Add clusters of lamium and pulmonaria with their splotched and spotted beauty, a soupçon of shrubs such as viburnums, magnolia and dogwood, and this becomes one of the most exciting parts of the garden all year round.

Hellebores take a long time to establish themselves — about three years here — but then grow to amazing proportions and flower profusely. One of the main reasons I like to creep slowly around the garden in spring is to look into the faces of these complex plants. What you assume are flowers are really sepals. Get out a magnifying glass, and you can see the real flowers deep inside. Framing the sepals are the bracts (the little green leaf-shapes). Now all of this had me consulting an encyclopedia, which is what every

The garden of haute spring in all its glory. I try to keep the bulbs flowing to echo the river-like path around the berm. This is a fantasy, of course, and each year I put in hundreds of plants where I can find any place at all for them. The red-foliaged plant in the centre is a Japanese maple, *Acer palmatum* 'Dissectum Atropurpureum'. It has been in this spot from the beginning of the garden's renovation. To the right of it in full bloom is *Daphne* x *burkwoodii* 'Somerset' and, below that, the creamy bottlebrush flowers of dwarf *Fothergilla gardenii*. Both are so fragrant we can smell them on the deck. At the lower right, a variegated boxwood, *Buxus sempervirens* 'Aureovariegata', puts on its bright new leaves. The small purple rhododendron, *R.* 'Ramapo', clashes horribly with the maple but I can't move either of them so I just put up with it.

good gardener needs. Learning the parts of plants is fun, and the hellebore is a terrific one to practice on. And I discover, there are two kinds of hellebore: caulescent (flowering stems — floral bracts, leaves and flowers on one stem — with thin, wiry roots) and acaulescent (multistemmed with thick, fleshy roots).

The translucent white bracts of *Helleborus niger* (acaulescent) with pure gold stamens are worth the wait. *H. atrorubens* has a dramatic ruby-red bloom that must be very carefully placed to show it off properly. All hellebores are adaptable plants. The colder the area, the later they bloom. *H. niger* (the roots are black) is called the Christmas rose in Europe because that is when it flowers there. Here, it's more likely to bloom in April. *H. orientalis*, the Lenten rose, supposedly because it comes out 40 days before Easter, has never shown up that early. Its distinctive speckled throat is charming; it has a wide range of colors and will self-seed, but not to any great extent in this garden.

H. foetidus, stinking hellebore (caulescent), is a native of southwest Europe with fan-shaped leaves and pale green bells edged in maroon. This is a real stunner and looks especially good combined with brunnera for a strong contrast in shape and foliage color. Hellebores love dappled shade and lots of humus and will thrive in moist soil. I have never tried to move any of them; I'm told they object to this.

There are good losses and bad losses in gardening. A purple-leaf sand cherry looked awful and was quickly given away. But a birch tree that succumbed to the dreaded borer was definitely a sad loss. It had grown in the center toward the back for some 15 years. It was a great demarcation between the woodland and the back of the garden. This was a European birch (*Betula pendula*), and I didn't know about native birches when I planted it. Since I refused to have any lethal chemicals come into the garden, it eventually died. A native birch would have resisted bronze birch borer or fungus attack. When the birch died, so did a lot of illusions about what you can foist onto your land. The value of having a structure formed by native plants was made apparent. They will survive when other plants won't.

Planting, I found out early on, was not a matter of jamming some hapless creature into a tiny hole and hoping for the best. The usual result was a plant that got along, but just barely, and not nearly as well as those in better-prepared sites. Books tell you this sort of thing all the time; why, then, do we all have to go through the stage of thinking that it doesn't matter? Space, good watering and lots of top-dressing are the magic route to healthy plants. Time was wasted not doing this in the first place. And I still lash myself for the arrogance of ignoring this most basic principle.

At the same time, I quickly learned not to mess around with the soil. I wanted masses of plants. Cultivating, digging around plants, is fine in a huge vegetable garden, but not good in a small space.

Above left: *Helleborus atrorubens*. Above right: *Helleborus niger.* Hellebores are useful in just about any season. They will winter over with just a layer of mulch spread around them. I like this as a way to raise the profile of hybrids whose leaves will remain green. Some people like to cut the dying foliage away in spring; others leave it in place. I lean to the tidying-up side myself so I can see these magnificent faces more easily.

The woodland garden in spring is where I like to crawl around and get my face as close to the ground as possible. Never tidy up these areas because you could break the emerging head off some delicate plant. Above left: The Mayapple, *Podophyllum peltatum*, which develops a shiny, red fruit later in the season, is an eastern native. Above right: *Astilboides tabularis* is a great shade plant at its best in early spring. The leaves get quite large and are targets for anything falling from the weeping willow. Right: A small moment with a strange, pale-white hosta, which slugs will eat right to the ground. Beside it is yellow feverfew, *Tanacetum parthenium* 'Aureum'. It liberally self-seeds but is not nearly as invasive as the species. All around is creeping Jenny, *Lysimachia nummularia*, which *is* invasive; I have spent years pulling it out.

Cultivate as books implore, and you are discombobulating roots and well-balanced organic systems that don't need all that "help." I place compost around new plants, mulch as deeply as possible and let the worms do the rest of the work, aerating the soil and fertilizing it.

I became preoccupied with and then concerned about soil. Though this is the most basic stuff of human survival, it's breathtaking how casual and careless we can be about it, even in the garden. There are billions of minute forms of life below, from fungi to bacteria to protozoans to more familiar creatures such as worms and other creepy-crawlies. It seems we barely make their acquaintance before we want to drop some chemical or other on them. Yet each of these creatures plays a role in the health of the soil, we're not quite sure how, and each is a vital part of the biosphere, we're not sure why. We do know that when we interfere, we run the risk of upsetting a delicate balance somewhere. But that doesn't mean to say we can't improve the soil or keep it in good condition.

The most important part of the soil is humus, and while all humus is organic matter, not all organic matter is yet humus. This rich, dark stuff is organic matter that's gone through some form of decomposition. Manure and compost, leaves and kitchen wastes are organic matter, but they haven't yet reached the sophisticated stage of humus. This happens after the material is mixed with the soil and begins to break down, releasing essential minerals and nutrients.

It doesn't take a lot of work to maintain healthy soil. When digging new beds, I usually go down at least a foot and sometimes mix in compost or manure if the soil is poor. It will help develop good root systems. Otherwise, I top-dress. It may seem like a lazy way of going about things, this laissez-faire form of gardening, but it also means the vital life of the soil is left alone to carry on the job nature intended. Every time I put shovel to ground, I have this image of millions of dislocated beings.

In spring, my neighbors and I split the cost of several yards of good topsoil, which is put on spots that need some bumping up; it's absorbed like magic. It is absolutely necessary to find a reliable supplier because you don't want stuff that's filled with weed seeds or, worse, chemicals that render it lifeless. For heavy soil, also add a mix of coarse concrete sand and fine brick sand.

Spring is probably the most *cheerful* time of year. It's also when winter damage to plants becomes painfully clear. For woody plants with bark and twigs exposed to the elements, there are many dangers from the ravages of wind, sun and ice.

Winterkill, for instance, takes place when the temperature has dropped lower than a plant can cope with. If something woody hasn't ripened properly before winter comes on, twigs, tips or even whole branches can croak. Since I like to push the zones in my garden, a lot of things can look just fine when

This area is opposite the berm. I brought in an old chair long since out of commission just as something to plant around. The woodland section here changes almost annually because many of these plants are ruined by the flood. The burgundy foliage is *Lysimachia ciliata*; next to it is *Aquilegia* 'Nora Barlow'; the big leaf in the rear is *Petasites japonicus*; the variegated hosta is *H.* 'Frances Williams'; forward is *Thalictrum flavum*; below it is *Filipendula ulmaria* 'Aurea'. The large white leaves in the middle are *Pulmonaria* 'David Ward' with a mix of other pulmonarias, including 'Mrs. Moon', 'Excalibur' and 'Apple Frost', interplanted with the hostas 'Gold Edger' and 'Fragrant Gold'. A woodland phlox, *Phlox divaricata,* is the perfect foil to all this foliage.

The flowering shrubs of spring are brief but magnificent. Above left: Carolina silverbell, *Halesia carolina,* is not particularly distinguished the rest of the year but this moment is worth everything else. It will get to 25 feet but not in my lifetime. Above right: The earliest to come out is *Abeliophyllum distichum*, which is incorrectly called the white forsythia, I suppose because both plants bloom about the same time. I'll take this one over forsythia any time. Opposite: *Paeonia tenuifolia* has a brilliant, red flower which I'm not crazy about, but it only lasts for about ten minutes. I have this plant because the foliage is so splendid.

spring begins and then wilt for no apparent reason. In this case, the roots have died but enough energy is stored in the stem and branches that the plant will leaf out, even flower. But once that energy is exhausted, it's curtains.

Other things, however, can be killed right back to the ground but will resprout and live on and on because the roots have survived. It's hard not to get impatient when you see something that should be fine doing absolutely nothing. That's when the famous garden temperament (all mildness and persistence) has to come into play. Then one day, unpredictably, new growth erupts like magic from the base of what looked like a dead stick the day before. This is one very good reason never to pull anything out that hasn't looked like a corpse for at least a couple of years. You never know what action is going on in the root system. I usually cut out dead bits and pieces, and if a mild tug moves a plant easily, I know it's a goner.

Another problem to look out for is just how strong the sun is until trees have leafed out. This is a killer time of year for broadleaf evergreens such as mountain laurels, rhododendrons and *Pieris*, all of which can suffer from sunscald. Sun on the south side of a plant will activate its cells, then as the temperature plummets at night (as it often does in early spring), the cold can dry them out, which explains why so many of these plants look awful right now. They will eventually recover, but it usually means they should be in a more protected spot.

I don't worry too much about frost-cracking, which looks like fine cracks in the bark. The bark usually heals pretty quickly. But if it occurs year after year, scar tissue builds up and deep ridges form along the stem or branch of a plant. This will happen on the south or southwest side of a tree in late winter. The sun warms the bark during the day, and once the temperature nose-dives at night, the plant refreezes. Severe frost-cracking can result in deep, vertical splits in the wood, which are far more serious. They can be invaded by disease and lead to the plant's early demise. To avoid this damage, use a very dilute coat of white latex paint (10 parts water to 1 of paint) on vulnerable areas of the trunk and branches. This will reflect the sun's rays and prevent the plant from absorbing them. You can also loosely wrap the trunks of vulnerable plants such as Japanese maples with burlap to shade them.

Something I do worry about is the amount of salt that's tossed around our streets, getting splashed onto the plants in the front or walked into the back. Salt is toxic to plants. I've now got a pretty yew close to the front sidewalk. I keep a sharp eye on it in case the needles turn yellow or brown or there is twig dieback, all signs of damage. On deciduous trees, buds will shrivel up, and there will also be dieback or tangled twigs growing from one area (called a witches' broom). The trouble is that symptoms appear gradually and plants may be affected profoundly over a long period of time. But I hate the idea of using barriers

The riches of spring seem never to end and these plants prove it. Clockwise from top left: *Uvularia grandiflora* was given to me by a friend. I divide and move it around regularly, which seems to renew its vigor and size. You should never haul natives such as this out of the woodland unless their site is threatened. Only take a small sample. Siberian irises, *Iris sibirica*, probably need more sun than this shady section of the garden allows, but this particular plant seems to thrive. I keep it and the daylily behind under control by division every few years. *Brunnera macrophylla* 'Variegata' should never be permitted to dry out. Spanish bluebells, *Hyacinthoides hispanica*, are handsome May blooms that tolerate a fair whack of shade.

of burlap. There are other good plants that will stand up to these rigors of city pollution. (See the list of salt-tolerant plants at the end of the winter section.)

There have been years when entire beds have been undone by the freeze–thaw factor, and I have to start all over again. My mind says, "Great! Empty spots — room for new plants." My heart mourns the loss of even one plant.

The major mistake I made in the beginning was to put way too many plants in the same small area. That can guarantee lots of death. I didn't really take seriously the fact that size on a label means something. When it says "grows to 8 feet," the plant probably will, and more in a protected site. Spread is also a major consideration in a small garden. I've certainly miscalculated that on occasion. For instance, a wonderful *Daphne* x *burkwoodii* 'Somerset', a little stick of a thing about 18 inches high, was planted in one of the soil squares around the middle of the checkerboard. Lovely plant with variegated leaves that hang on most of the winter, a pleasant, bowl-like shape, and blossoms in spring and autumn that give off a scent we can smell on the deck. Daphnes grow to 5 feet and spread to 3 feet. Ignoring this, I planted a *Viburnum plicatum* 'Summer Snowflake' right next to it. What a combination, I thought, both with gorgeous spring blooms; one with vibrant autumn leaves backed by the less intense green of the other.

This viburnum flowers all summer long, so of course it's important to be able to see the lacecap blooms easily. But it grows to 6 feet and spreads at least 4 feet. When the plants reached maturity, I had a choice: move the viburnum and risk killing it, or keep pruning for its special role. It gets pruned. I like the combination much too much, and it's the price of bad planning.

Planning is always a good idea in a complex garden. I'd love to have a design set down, but I've found over the years that no matter how many new drawings I make during the winter, what dictates the action are winter deaths and the plants available in nurseries.

But I can plan. I can plan to take out a tree and release light into a dark area. I can plan to remove something that's been in the garden too long, done its duty and needs to be put down if not out. What I usually plan is what I'm going to do in spring.

I have a list of plants that didn't really perform well the previous year. I dither about whether to take them out, usually decide to leave them alone for just one more year, then add them to next year's list of Things To Do. The red tulips are a case in point. They always seemed spotty and, in such a confined space, rather like over-dressed tarts on parade, not the painterly sweep of color I really had in mind. I finally solved the problem — red is hard to place — by moving them to the very back, and it's a bonus to see them off in the distance clumped together. Great for cutting.

Here's a combination I find riveting in and out of season. The stripy foliage of *Polemonium caeruleum* 'Brise d'Anjou' made it the hot plant at the time I installed it. It goes well with the sweet woodruff, *Galium odoratum*, when it is in bloom. The fascinating foliage in the background is *Berberis thunbergii* 'Atropurpurea Nana' which I bought at a special plant sale and now wish were more generally available. The red foliage and glossy leaves become more intense in autumn.

Narcissus are the backbone of my spring garden. I usually keep them in groups so they form a good background for small bulbs, or I bunch them up to make a bouquet. They should be planted in areas where the sun will hit them before overhead leaves have completely unfurled. They love well-drained soil so haven't done very well along the edges of the berm. Keep their planting areas covered with leaf mould and never touch them in spring. The colder the area, the stronger the flower.

Opposite left: *Narcissus* 'Cheerfulness' is a bit frilly for my more austere moments, but it is also highly scented. Opposite right: *N.* 'Jack Snipe' is one of the little forms I find so appealing. Above left: *N.* 'Thalia' is everywhere in my garden. I love the pure white of the graceful, drooping blooms. The dark shadow near it is *Fritillaria meleagris*. Above right: *N.* 'Tête-à-Tête' is another small narcissus that will tuck in almost anywhere. Try narcissus with hellebores, near hostas (which will hide the yellowing foliage) and with other woodland plants that bloom slightly later in the season.

Fritillarias, or frits as they are often called, have a sense of humor in the tilt of their bells. Plant them in sunny spots in autumn and make sure the bulbs aren't dried out when you buy them. Above left: *F. meleagris* has solitary checkered flowers and grows to 15 inches. Above right: *F. michailovskyi* with its strange-looking, yellow and purple flower always excites visitors. Opposite: *Nectaroscordum siculum* is a member of the allium family but differs in that it has outer petals with three to five veins where alliums have only one. It grows about 4 feet tall and has magnificent bells that open up at the top of the stem. Rumored to be invasive. I only wish. I have it here with *Euphorbia dulcis* 'Chameleon' which perfectly picks up the burgundy in its flower.

Spring-flowering clematis are a must. They tend to be smaller and more interesting than the big-flowered hybrids which will come along later in the season. I gravitated toward the small-flowered species recently simply because they never used to be available. Above left is *C. alpina* 'Willy' and above right is *C. montana* 'Elizabeth'. These forms, which will scramble up a trellis or a tree, need to be cut back after flowering.

This is also the time when I get out and clean up my collection of secateurs (one can never have too many). I get into whacking-back mode with practically the first light of spring. This impulse must be curbed. To satisfy my twitchy fingers, I take out all the dead stuff and anything obviously diseased from vines, roses and any shrubs that have started to leaf out. There are some things that will leap forward by being pruned early. I'm thinking of *Clematis x jackmanii*, which likes to be cut back to good, thick buds about a foot off the ground. For large, fresh purple leaves on the smoke tree, *Cotinus coggygria*, chop it back hard to about three buds from the base; same with elders and spireas. Other summer-flowering shrubs such as kerria, rose of Sharon, tamarisk, hypericums and some hydrangeas can also be pruned now.

But plants such as maples and birches must be left alone. With the exception of buddleias, I resist any temptation to have a go at silver-foliaged plants such as artemisia, lavender, *Caryopteris* or *Perovskia*. It's much better to wait until there are signs of growth near the base before cutting them back. I hold off until very late May or early June. They all bloom on new wood, and tidying them up too soon runs the risk of bumping them off. Putting up with a little raggedness now pays off later in large, healthy plants.

Spring is also the time for very serious dividing and moving around. Some woody plants should be moved only in the spring; these include magnolia, dogwood, holly, Japanese maple and most viburnums. Apart from these, I happily transplant things right up until the end of September. Not foolishly, not in a heat wave and not if I know there'll be a frost. These are early-morning tasks, and I water everything very deeply, then add a thick mulch. Often, however, this is done in such a flurry that it leaves me done in for weeks and the idea of quality maintenance seems like a rest. Someone once described my garden as plants on the move. But it's fun to do this. And what, after all, is gardening except fun?

My most perfect time in the Jardin des Refusés is when these two plants are opened up together; I actually sit down and enjoy. Above left is *Viburnum plicatum tomentosum* 'Shasta' and above right is *Rosa hugonis* or Father Hugo's rose. They are underplanted with *Allium* 'Purple Sensation', and I find it all breathtaking. Opposite: The Jardin des Refusés has developed over the years into a really pleasant place to be. It is sunny until early afternoon and there's just enough light to support roses. In this area, there are densely prickled rugosas, a number of the hardy 'Explorer' series, and the ever-blooming shrub rose, 'The Fairy'.

spring tips

clean-up

- Use boiling water to get rid of weeds around stones and in paths.
- Scrape off winter mulch once big bulbs have made an appearance and return it to the compost.
  Wait until new growth is well on its way before adding spring mulch.
- Don't start spraying with chemicals.
  No matter what the label tells you, if it says to keep away from fish, birds and other animals, it's poison.
- Mulch to a depth of about 3 inches around tree bases, keeping well away from the bark.
- Spring is a good time to fertilize. I tend to use sheep manure mixed with compost.
- Hellebores and most other perennials like manure tea: 20 parts water to 1 part manure, with 1 teaspoon
  of blood meal mixed in for good measure. Store in a cool, dark place and use within a few weeks.

pruning

- Pruning shifts the concentration of energy from one part of the plant to another.
  Cut off the tip of a branch or a bud, and that energy will move to the nearest bud.
- Cut out anything dead or diseased on trees and shrubs any time of the year.
- Start serious spring pruning when you see buds start to form.
- If you want a branch or twig to grow to the right, find a bud pointing to the right
  and cut off whatever is growing above or beyond it.
- Always make smooth cuts, using very sharp tools cleaned with denatured alcohol.
- I leave most vines alone, taking out any dead material and trimming back for length or shape.
  Don't hesitate to cut back rampant vines severely.
- Wisteria blooms on new wood and should be done twice a year. Late winter: Always prune with a form
  in mind. Choose what will be the main branches, and then cut all side shoots back to the first four buds.
  If you reprune in June, again being careful not to cut off buds, chances are it will bloom again.
- Early-flowering clematis such as *C. montana*, *C. alpina* and *C. macropetala* bloom on last year's growth.
  Wait until after they've bloomed. Cut out what's dead or damaged and trim back.
  Early, large-flowering cultivars also grow on last year's branches. Leave them alone.
- Hybrids (such as *Clematis x jackmanii*) produce flowers on new stems. Cut back to what looks like a major
  stem about 12 inches from the ground.
- Forsythia blooms on old wood; trim it and other spring-flowering shrubs after blooming,
  removing the oldest stems at ground level.
- Cut out any suckers around lilacs.
- Don't touch maples, walnuts or birches until later in the season.
- If you've planted new trees, make sure to trim off enough of the top growth to compensate
  for any roots that might have been lost in transplanting.

Bloodroot
Brunnera
Daphne
Erythronium
Hellebores
Japanese maple
Magnolia
Muscari
Pulmonaria
Scilla
Serviceberry
Solomon's seal
Species tulips

stars of spring

summer

The first long days of summer
drift into the garden
around six in the morning.

It's when the garden is at its most ravishing, backlit by the sun rising over the neighboring houses and the huge old trees. I always think it can never be this glorious again. I'm always wrong.

Each garden has its own special times. Dawn is one of them for mine, another is at the end of the day, when the sunset (which we cannot see for houses) is reflected off the ample canopy of the weeping willow. The light floods between the plants, etching them to perfection, making them almost stand out in relief. These are my happiest hours, when there is nothing but contentment. This is the role of the garden in my life.

To decide what you want of a garden requires knowing a lot about yourself. Your style will have an enormous influence — gardening begins with a fair amount of baggage. My garden is better looked after than my house, mainly because the garden interests me more than interior decorating or wearing fashionable clothes. So the garden became the place with the real style.

I'm an inveterate collector. Paintings, old glass, flow-blue dishes, bits and bobs picked up in junk stores are my excuses for home furnishing. The garden slowly but naturally took on the same feel. It's full of stuff ranging from containers collected over the years to old watering cans, grills that serve a number of purposes from holding up vines to just being a small moment on a fence almost smothered in greenery. Having all these objects scattered about also gives the garden a sense of being lived in and cherished. I would never dream of cleaning these things up, but I do move them around regularly as it takes my fancy. It's the garden, not my house, that's full of romance and poetry.

Making plants happy is a major part of gardening: Growing things well becomes more and more important the older I get. I hate even the concept of "low-maintenance" or "no-care" gardening. That's window dressing, not gardening. What we do is very focused on making things look beautiful and creating a tranquil refuge. Both of these may be a subtext, but plants come first.

Know your plants, and know your site. Having a sense of place in the garden is significant. It means feeling comfortable in a familiar spot where every mood is intimately known. It is like having an affair, and you want to try your best to seduce this quirky lover whose good will is at the caprice of the weather.

On these long summer days, I spend as many hours as possible among the plants composing what I hope are pleasing scenes. As well, there is always something to be divided or some plant(s) still sitting on the deck waiting to be placed. This becomes a particular trick in a crowded garden. Making choices is part of the pleasure; finding space is part of the problem. I like to walk around the garden with a plant much the way my garden heroines Vita Sackville-West and Gertrude Jekyll did in the past. It seems a natural way to arrange plant positions and make up new combinations.

Midsummer on the berm makes me want to curl up amid the sensuality of these lush leaves. This shows what a range of color and texture there is in foliage. The burgundy leaves in the background belong to a redbud, *Cercis canadensis* 'Forest Pansy', replacing the birch tree which succumbed to disease. It looks a bit naked there now but in a few years this will fill out nicely. The huge hosta to the left is 'Sum and Substance' and it will get to be enormous; from the grasses forward are the hostas 'Gold Standard,' 'Halcyon', 'Hadspen Blue' and over to the left is 'August Moon'. The foliage on the berm includes brunnera, the deep green of hellebores and the glossy, heart-shaped leaf of European ginger, *Asarum europaeum.*

Woody plants have been added by the dozens to the garden over the years. Even a small space can accommodate shrubs of various sizes. Left: Early summer brings forth the creamy flower clusters of leatherleaf viburnum, *Viburnum rhytidophyllum* 'Allegheny', a good screening plant that stays evergreen almost all winter here. Above left: *Fothergilla gardenii* starts in spring and carries on for weeks in June. Above right: Oakleaf hydrangea, *Hydrangea quercifolia,* is a great plant with exfoliating bark, wonderful lacecap bloom and foliage that turns a tarnished burgundy-red in autumn. It asks only for dappled shade and moisture.

Most of these shrubs require little care except to see that they are planted properly and don't dry out. All need decent drainage. Above left: *Enkianthus campanulatus* lasted for many years but was bumped off by budding out before the last hard frost, so this is its memorial. A wonderful, vase-shaped plant that survived in well-drained clay soil though it needs a little acid. Above right: This mountain laurel, *Kalmia latifolia* 'Shooting Star', survived a branch from the willow falling on it. I put lots of pine needles around it for mulch. Right: *Rosa hugonis* and *Viburnum plicatum tomentosum* 'Shasta' carry on from spring right into summer.

Measure texture against texture, see what leaf shapes complement or contrast with each other and picture how they might look together. Imagine the color of a bloom in the mind's eye, and figure out how well it will sit with what's already there. Being deliberate is very important. Plopping plants in helter-skelter just to get them in the ground is mere landscaping and has nothing to do with the intimacy real gardening affords.

Combining plants from wildly disparate regions — a mountain plant with a desert plant, for example — will, eventually, seem odd. To avoid this means learning where a plant comes from and a bit about its background. At first, this might seem like learned lumber, but in the long run, it helps make good choices.

On the other hand, this doesn't mean you're allowed to have only Mediterranean plants in one place. They will look absolutely right, of course, and since all have the same soil, light and watering requirements, they will be easy to maintain. There are no rules carved in stone, but a rudimentary logic says that this makes sense. Until, that is, you get a better idea and want to throw something into the mix that's outrageous or wonderful (and that likes the same growing conditions).

Investigate roots by teasing them out of the pot and giving them a sniff, sizing up just how much (or little) space they can put up with, and what kind of light will make the plant thrive. Plant culture includes all these things as well as pedigree. If it's an alpine, it will want well-drained, lean soil and will be close to the ground, but if it's from the forests of China or Oregon, the rich hush of a woodland would be more appropriate.

Reading about plant origins becomes second nature after a few years of gardening. It's a pleasure to learn about the history of a plant and why it got its name (usually something as sensible as the fact that the Hooker family or the Tradescants found it on their travels and brought it into the trade). From there, it's easy to figure out what will make a plant flourish.

I make a lot of mistakes. Dozen of plants have died; more have been clumsily placed. Every time something like this happens, there's a lesson. Creeping Jenny, *Lysimachia nummularia*, is an effective groundcover that spreads swiftly, has a yellow flower in spring and will grow in the shade. It is aggressive, and since its job of holding soil in place on the berm was finished, I've spent years pulling it out.

Another member of this rampant family is the gooseneck loosestrife, *Lysimachia clethroides*. This white-blooming plant starts out slowly and is well-behaved for about two years. I adored it until it took off, bouncing its way where it wasn't wanted. Getting it out is a matter of persistence. It looks fine in big drifts in a country garden, but beware of it in a very small city garden. *L. punctata* is, again, too pushy for the city. Keep it in the country, where its streams of yellow blooms will look great. The one lysimachia I do like is *L. ciliata* 'Purpurea'. It starts out with deep burgundy foliage and greens up during the season, then concentrates on producing attractive yellow flowers. It may run a bit, but it's easy to keep in check.

The garden was designed to rise as the seasons progress. Here it is in summer with a smattering of blossoms. On the extreme left is the white form of *Sidalcea malviflora* which I keep deadheaded so it will keep going. Behind is a white phlox, *P. maculata* 'Miss Lingard', and the dotting about of blue is a *Geranium pratense* that went to seed from the year before. It's easy enough to keep it pulled out. In the center of the picture is a *Ginkgo biloba* which replaced an ailing maple. I had the latter chopped down when all my neighbors were at their cottages. Suddenly, things shot up and I now use the stump as a plinth for an old Chinese jar. On the right in the foreground is a stunning coralbark maple, *Acer palmatum* 'Sango-kaku'.

Would I put creeping Jenny out again? Absolutely not. I'd find a series of groundcovers and let them duke it out with each other for space and to see what would look best with the plants coming after them. Now that I have so many good ones, I'm sorry I didn't know about them earlier. I'd certainly think of groundcovers for all four seasons. Spring would bring a brilliant blue swath of Dalmatian bellflower (*Campanula portenschlagiana*) or, on a more subtle note, sweet cicely (*Myrrhis odorata*), with lovely ferny leaves, seeding itself all over the place in shade as well as sun.

These are herbaceous plants. I'd mix them in with groundcovers of serious winter merit such as wintergreen, *Gaultheria procumbens*. It has white or pale pink flowers in summer, elliptical, glossy green leaves and scarlet berries in winter. Bearberry, *Arctostaphylos uva-ursi*, has white flowers followed by brilliant red berries. Wild ginger, *Asarum canadense,* is a deciduous plant with soft green leaves. Another must is the slow-spreading but absolutely stunning European ginger, *A. europaeum*. It has fine, rounded, shiny, evergreen leaves that will spring up in places where I'm sure I've not planted it— under the little Japanese maple, for instance.

There will always be plants that give some sort of trouble. This is unpredictable and can be quite different for every garden and gardener. My struggle is with geraniums. Hardy geraniums are, without doubt, splendid plants. They don't seem to have any diseases, they have different blooming times, and many are scented. Most respond to deadheading by blossoming on and on for weeks if not months. They have five-petaled flowers ranging from white to pink to brilliant, eye-popping magenta. But one that gets completely out of control is *Geranium pratense*. This is an attractive plant with blue flowers, the usual cut leaves, and stands about 18 inches high. I was sold this one as *G.* 'Johnson's Blue', a very desirable plant that grows in semishade and always looks good. Well, *G. pratense* is one of the parents, the one that self-seeds everywhere. Not knowing this, just once, I was too casual with deadheading and ended up with what looked like a geranium farm. Not what I intended. I want lots of plants but not all the same ones. It's now a constant battle to root it out.

Many years later, I asked one of my favorite nurserymen if he could guarantee that he was actually selling me *G.* 'Johnson's Blue'. Nope, was the reply. No one can, he told me, we just hope, even though they're still labeled this way. You'll know you have it if doesn't seed all over the place. Until then, just keep pulling out *G. pratense*, enjoy the blooms and know you'll never completely get rid of it.

Another fecund little geranium is *G.* x *oxonianum* 'Claridge Druce' (a cross between *G. endressii* and *G. versicolor*). The new seedlings are even more vigorous than the parent and will pop up in sun or shade.

I am partial to the smaller geraniums, and the one I like best of all is *G. renardii*. It stands 8 inches high, has a rounded, dimpled leaf with purple-veined white flowers. It doesn't get straggly or rampant,

I suspect this peony was old when we bought our house in 1967. You see this one in farm and city gardens across the country. It might be *Paeonia* 'Sarah Bernhardt' which has been around for a while or, more likely, one that was simply labelled 'Pink' in a long-forgotten nursery. Whatever it is, I love it and have divided and moved it around to a fare-thee-well over all these years. Nothing seems to daunt it. Now, it's in the Jardin des Refusés on my neighbor's side next to a *Petasites japonicus* (highly invasive but splendid foliage). I cut the peony blooms when they are young, let them dry out and put them in arrangements.

Summer seems to demand strong colors and this gallery contains some of the best. Above left: *Angelica gigas* will get to at least 5 feet and retain this intense purple shade in its leaves and dramatic 4-inch umbels. Above right: *Knautia macedonica* is a fantastic plant with just about the deepest tone of burgundy possible. I like it teamed with the lacy leaves of *Tamarix ramosissima*, a plant known for its wonderful, feathery foliage. I hate the flowers of this plant which emerge in the vilest pink, like cheap underwear. I whack them off and keep it nicely pruned. It goes well with grasses and a great plant like the knautia.

Above left: A glorious combination that surprises me each year. The *Ajuga reptans* 'Burgundy Glow' moves about the stones, popping up here and there and finally resting with the golden *Hakonechloa macra* 'Aureola'. This is my favorite grass. It is so well behaved and its cascading form works well as an edger, in containers or placed with other plants. It appreciates a bit of shade. In full sun, the color bleaches out. Above right: *Salvia verticillata* 'Spring Rain' will stay in this pristine condition for weeks on end. Backing it up is a golden elder, *Sambucus canadensis* 'Aurea', which should be pruned back hard each spring.

There are some really lovely native North American plants and among the best is *Anemone canadensis* (above left), but it will travel the length and breadth of a garden if allowed. I keep it confined to a couple of plants and am reconciled to pulling it out forever. There are self-seeding forget-me-nots in the background. Above right: One of the 'Explorer' series, *Rosa* 'Henry Hudson', puts up with low light values and sits happily with *Clematis montana* var. *wilsonii*. Opposite: This is a stunner *Rubus rosifolius* 'Coronarius' and I've got it near *Acer palmatum* 'Scolopendrifolium' and what may, foolishly, be *Oxydendrum*, a native tree that will grow to 25 feet.

staying in a handsome cluster all season. *G. sanguineum* is one highly effective front-of-border geranium. It has a delicate pink flower, and when cut back fiercely, the foliage will make a voluptuous mound. I also like *G. macrorrhizum* 'Album'. I think this form is superior to the species, which has such a difficult hue of magenta touched with orange that it's tricky to place. I have the species next to an azalea of dazzling cerise. When they are in bloom, I wear blinkers to get past them the clash is so extreme. This geranium spreads like crazy. I've tended to give up pulling it out because the ghastliness lasts for only a week and the foliage provides great autumn color, which is one of the main reasons to have it. *G. m.* 'Album', on the other hand, doesn't spread so quickly and has the same good foliage. This is a wonderful plant to cover up really nasty areas where nothing else will grow.

I find other geraniums will flop about in the most disorganized way. Some, such as *Geranium phaeum,* grow well in the shade, get to about 3 feet and have small but rather pretty granny-bonnet-type flowers. I found it disappointing in my garden, although I'd seen it looking great in other people's. I experimented with *G. p. album* and *G. p.* 'Raven', both of which I like much better than old *G. phaeum*. All work extremely well as space fillers among other tallish plants.

I have *G. p. album* and *G. p.* 'Raven' near a huge *Lavatera* 'Barnsley' that looks best with things clustered around it. Backing this lot up is *Boltonia asteroides*, which would normally get to about 8 feet. It looks fabulous in autumn with a magnificent shower of white aster-like blooms. Of course, it will break in half during the first big wind. Forgo some of the height and cut it back somewhat in July.

I say somewhat because I'm never sure just how much you should nip anything back. It depends on your taste and how big you ultimately want the plant to get. Asters and chrysanthemums respond to pinching back by a third at the end of July. This usually makes for a neater plant later on. I always let mine go, which means they end up looking scraggly. But I do curtail the boltonia, and I love the results at 6 feet. This group, *Boltonia*, *Lavatera* and *Geranium*, has a smaller *Tradescantia* 'Concord Grape' clutching at its skirts. It is the most amazing shade of purple and stands out brilliantly against all that imploding green.

How to place big plants is always a quandary, no matter what size the garden. From the beginning of my renovation, I knew I didn't want a conventional garden based on the principle of big plants at the back and little ones in front. Since my biggies are dotted all about the place creating smokescreens from one section to the next, I don't really worry except when they shade out plants to the rear. When this happens, I hope the plants behind will carry on growing very slowly and eventually make their own statements. This doesn't always work, but it's successful often enough to keep encouraging me to plant this way. Undulations everywhere.

Hardy geraniums are charming plants, especially when they have faces as pure and simple as these. Above left is *Geranium macrorrhizum* 'Ingwersen's Variety', a wonderful cultivar. The species is a major groundcover but it has a magenta flower I can't deal with. I like this one much better. Above right: *G. sylvaticum* 'Album' is a neat little plant that grows to 10 inches here. Both have good autumn foliage and the leaves have a faintly medicinal scent.

Above left: This is a very pleasing combination. *Achillea* 'Snow Taler' will even grow in a slightly shady area. In the rear is the best of all foliage plants, *Artemisia* x 'Huntington'. The blue is from a container of the annual fairy fanflower, *Scaevola aemula* 'Blue Wonder'. Above right: *Perovskia atriplicifolia*, commonly known as Russian sage, is one of the soldiers of the midsummer garden, though it does tend to flop once it reaches maturity. The airiness it brings to the garden is emphasized in the picture on the right where it's combined with the similarly blue-and-silver *Caryopteris* x *clandonensis*. In the background is another stalwart, *Eupatorium rugosum* 'Chocolate'. All three plants have blooms that persist for weeks and weeks.

This gives my garden a look of being free and loose, which of course it isn't. It is very organized but designed (if that's not too fancy a term for the way I plant) to look as casual as possible. I'm always moving things about in the summer to make sure that the look persists and that the garden has a perpetual sense of exuberance. A tall plant at the front or even in the middle of a border will break up a dull patch and slow down the eye as it wanders along. A very large plant anchoring a border can provide a focal point. So I use all these methods of making garden transitions. Eclectic is my middle name.

Meadow rue, *Thalictrum*, is one of the lanky ones I wouldn't be without. It has almost lacy leaves with blooms that range from yellow (*T. flavum*) to a dark lavender (*T. rochebruneanum* and *T. aquilegiifolium*). The latter is my favorite because the leaves really are like aquilegias and they stay a deep blue-gray all season.

Another tall one, meadowsweet, *Filipendula ulmaria* 'Aurea', looks particularly good in the woodland and has a huge puff of white flowers for most of the summer. There's a variegated form that even I, a lover of variegation, found too weird. Though I wouldn't get rid of it, I had to put it in with other bizarre-looking plants and fob them off as my Weird Section.

Although I've since broken up the Weird Section, I am partial to variegated plants. But they must be used with a great deal of taste and a lot of caution. Variegated plants are usually an anomaly in a species and have been bred specifically for the variegation. They tend, for that reason, to be on the delicate side. Many do better in some shade rather than full sun.

Variegation can bring luminosity to a dull area and add some real zip to a combination. I like fitting in variegations with what I'd consider placid plants — a plain hosta, for example, which will look smashing against a striped grass. A variegated iris, *I. pallida* 'Variegata', with the ferny lace of an artemisia can work anywhere. A gold-splashed dogwood, *Cornus florida* 'Welchii', adds punctuation and drama to a group of evergreens and low-growing shrubs.

Whatever is done with variegation, the key word is moderation. I once put together a whole border of variegated plants, and it looked like a hospital ward. The splotches, splashes, stripes and edgings of silver and gold were a true eyesore when all jammed together. Once I moved most of them on to other places, the improvement was instant. Many of them were pulmonarias. Now, this is a plant I am crazy about. And two together is enough: the pale green and white of *Pulmonaria rubra* 'David Ward' with the blue and silver of *P. longifolia* 'Bertram Anderson' is about as extreme as I want to get.

One of the best discoveries I've made is *Eupatorium*. The versions we find in the nurseries are related to the good old Joe-Pye weed found in the ditches and any other mildly damp depressions in the countryside. I have one that gets to 15 feet tall on a good year. It looks as though it's been on steroids,

Lacy, see-through plants are important in any garden. You can slip either of the above plants in almost anywhere to fill in holes and add an airy dimension. Above left is *Filipendula ulmaria*, which will take partial shade and grows from 3 to 5 feet high. On the right is *Thalictrum delavayi* 'Hewitt's Double', just a great plant that grows to about 4 feet. Many thalictrums will seed about but it's not a serious problem.

I tried a whole border of yellow and blue plants with varying success. If you are going to do something like this, you have to work with the foliage first and foremost. This little duet (above left) of *Lysimachia nummularia* 'Aurea' and bleeding heart, *Dicentra* 'Langtrees', is simple but effective. Similarly (above right), the golden grass, *Hakonechloa macra* 'Aureola', contrasts with *Astilbe* 'Sprite'. Opposite: Undulations of greenery show that it's not necessary to have a lot of blooms to make a garden highly textured and sensual. In the centre is *Acer palmatum* 'Sango-kaku', which will eventually screen out the buildings in the background. To its left is a variegated boxwood and, in the foreground, clusters of white *Phlox paniculata* 'Mt. Fuji'.

and I've done nothing particular to it. The huge blooms are like giant pale pink ghosts rising above all the other plants. The flower heads are often a foot across. I've sometimes stood under one and watched at least a dozen butterflies sucking or dozing. You can easily find *E. maculatum* and *E. purpureum*, which range in height from 4 to 12 feet.

The most useful in the family, to my mind, is *Eupatorium rugosum* 'Chocolate'. It stays at 4 feet and forms nice clumps without unbridled girth. The leaves remain a deep burgundy all season, making a marvelous background for other, more delicate foliage. Then in the autumn as the white flowers start to open, the leaves turn a deep green. It blooms and blooms for almost six weeks. I think it's impossible to place some plants badly — this is one of them. With such a plant as this dotted through the garden, designing is a cinch. Start with one of these, add a few more incrementally and you've got a moment, a scene and the beginning of a picture.

I have it as a background to huge pots of coleus in deep pink and magenta shades, and it tones them down nicely. In another spot, it's the foil for a variegated hydrangea. The crisp leaves in both cases make a fine, tailored combination. In yet another place, it stands next to a cut-leaf dwarf birch, *Betula pendula* 'Trost's Dwarf', providing a strong contrast to the ethereal leaves of this little tree.

When you try to divide or move these large, leafy plants in summertime, take care. Dig a hole deep enough and large enough to accommodate lots of native soil around the root ball. Make sure the soil in the hole is well-worked and watered deeply before putting in the plant. There will be some moping, but it will come back to life quickly and may even bloom again, though I never count on this. I suppose it's possible to prop up big plants, but I hate seeing a forest of bamboo stakes and tend to put big plants close together so they can lean on one other.

Using skinny plants helps this along. And there are none skinnier or more exciting than alliums. Members of the onion family, they have long, elegant scapes (or stems), strap-like foliage and flower clusters that range from pure white to yellow to rosy pink to pale blue to deep purple. Wander through a garden decked out with alliums, and a faint, pleasant scent of onion hangs in the air. You can be a serious collector of alliums because there are about 700 species divided into ornamental and edible. The latter includes *Allium schoenoprasum*, ordinary garden chives. Apart from being good to eat just as it is breaking open, the rich lilac bloom makes a good cut flower.

Allium tuberosum, garlic chives, grows in sturdy clumps with star-like white flowers that attract bees, butterflies and all sorts of other good insects. They bloom for weeks during the summer and are nonpareil for the vase, but you have to watch this one like a hawk. If it goes to seed, you end up with a field of them.

Sidalceas are such good value, I am tempted to add a lot more to this area. The pink one (top left) is *S. malviflora*; the white (top right) is *S. candida*. The racemes of funnel-shaped flowers come on in midsummer and, if kept deadheaded, last for weeks. Lower left: *Rudbeckia nitida* 'Herbstsonne' hits a towering 7 feet and is like a shower of gold in August. It also attracts aphids (little red suckers) which in turn attract lady bugs. Lower right: Monkshood, *Aconitum*, is a brooding plant (and poisonous, by the way) with a stunning color. It comes in not only this glorious blue (*A. napellus*) but also white and pale ivory. I do nothing with this plant and it always looks great. It will grow in semi-shade and makes a good cut flower.

This is fine as a filler where bulbs have left serious gaps. Divide any form of chives every few years to keep them healthy and under control.

Ornamental alliums are incredibly versatile, with heights ranging from 8 inches to 6 feet. They slip in between other plants with great ease and make good companions for either medium-sized groundcovers such as sweet woodruff (*Galium odoratum*), spotted deadnettle (*Lamium maculatum*) and lungwort (*Pulmonaria angustifolia*) or almost any tall, slender plants on a similar scale. They need sun and well-drained soil and should be planted in a hole two to three times as deep as the height of the bulb. Place in clusters rather than dotting them about. Keep size in mind. I speak from experience, as I look at all sorts of pretty little ones completely obscured by much larger plants. You shouldn't have to work hard to be able to see plants.

I adore the small ones such as *Allium flavum*, a delicious yellow about 8 inches high, and the pink *A. roseum*. Slightly taller is *A. moly*, an exquisite, adaptable little thing with brilliant yellow flowers useful in a formal border or a lightly shaded woodland or rockery. It looks gorgeous with the blue of *Geranium pratense* and yarrow such as *Achillea* 'Moonshine'. Beware, however: It will spread itself about with gay abandon.

I've grown dozens and dozens of *Allium* 'Purple Sensation', which in my garden comes out at the end of May and goes on well into June. It has stiff, leafless gray-blue stems about 3 feet high, topped with purple, lollipop-like balls 6 inches in diameter. Combine it with tulips and irises.

In June, *A. caeruleum*, which grows to 2 feet, connects with *Alchemilla mollis*, lady's mantle. The cornflower blue of the allium with the velvety green leaves and acid yellow of the lady's mantle is sublime. *Nectaroscordum siculum* subsp. *bulgaricum* used to be called *A. bulgaricum* but is now recognized as a relative. I mention this because it's a spectacular plant with bell-shaped off-white blooms flushed with purple and pink that drip from a central point on 4-foot stems. This one needs a bit of shade and also comes out in June. It does best in warmer areas. I have it rising over *Euphorbia dulcis* 'Chameleon' and *Hakonechloa macra* 'Aureola', one of the best of all ornamental grasses. This is one of the most satisfying combinations I have.

A. christophii (syn. *A. albopilosum*), star-of-Persia, is as enchanting as its common name. It has 18-inch scapes and huge spheres of metallic purple that sprong out like a child's sparkler. Tucked among large perennials, the flower heads look dramatic almost all day and then turn into dark blobs at night, so putting them next to silver or gray foliage or plants with white blooms makes for a captivating effect. I've also planted them near a dwarf lilac and other spring-flowering shrubs. The alliums appear to come from the branches of the shrubs and give the illusion of an extended season of bloom.

This is a view looking back from the compost area. It gives an idea of how densely the garden is planted. I've been slowly accumulating ferns of all types and promptly losing the identifications. The same can be said of the hosta, which might well be *H.* 'Regal Splendor', dominating the picture. It's been divided up so often it has become one of the punctuation marks of the garden. I'm not crazy about the flowers of any hosta and use them in arrangements rather than see their gawky spikes poking up over all the place.

Later on, there is nothing finer than *Allium sphaerocephalum*, an opulent purple on 3-foot scapes, or *A. cernuum*, another July–August beauty. The bell-shaped flowers are suspended like drops of liquid pink crystal. Combine it with poker-faced plants such as gayfeather (*Liatris*) or late-blooming lilies in the same tone and height for an eye-stopping display.

While alliums provide a kind of droll quality for the summer garden, romance and moonlight can be had with silver and gray plants artfully woven throughout. My outright favorite is *Artemisia* x 'Huntington'. It's a magnificent shrub-sized silver plant hardy enough to come through the winter. If not, a season's growth will make it plump and frothy. It stays looking fairly full most of the year, although any artemisia looks like wet laundry after being exposed to the cold for a while. *A.* x 'Powis Castle' and *A. absinthium* 'Lambrook Silver' are two more shrubby artemisias, smaller than 'Huntington', and although they haven't been tough survivors in my garden, I keep adding them every year for the sheer pleasure of their company.

Just about any artemisia can play many valuable roles: they harmonize colors, back up strong tints and, in our North American light, bring more freshness to a garden than almost any other plant. They have a calming effect and can subdue brilliant colors. Artemisias will knit one area with another and add an interesting contrast in foliage textures. Since it's important to repeat colors for unity, these are the ones I'd choose as most useful. In drought conditions, they hold up better than many other plants. They are also the buttress for any good combination of woody plants: for instance, *A.* x 'Huntington' with *Sedum* 'Möhrchen' and a variegated elder, *Sambucus nigra* 'Aureomarginata'. This triplet lives just off the deck, and they are so sensual, I want to be among them.

Artemisia ludoviciana 'Valerie Finnis' is the most intense of all silver plants, and it doesn't spread out recklessly like *A. l.* 'Silver King' and *A. l.* 'Silver Queen'. Those are so rampant, they will grow even in the shade, albeit slowly. Still, they are useful plants and can be used to great effect in containers. *A. lactiflora* is a statuesque plant that fits in readily with other tall plants. It blooms in late summer, when everything will get a lift from its frothy white panicles, and *A. l.* 'Guizho' is a stunner, with deeply notched leaves at the base.

My passion for gray and silver plants extends to shrubs and trees. The first time I saw a weeping silver pear, *Pyrus salicifolia* 'Pendula', was in a marvelous West Coast garden. It was just the most gorgeous thing I'd ever seen: gracefully arching branches covered with what almost looked like silver cobwebbing, the leaves were so delicate. Well, not sold where I live. I finally did track one down and had it shipped to a nursery outside town. A friend borrowed a truck and we collected it. It was a struggle getting this 10-foot tree into the garden, and normally I wouldn't buy such a large plant. I would rather have a small one and let it get acclimatized by growing into the garden. But since this was the only one there was, I had no choice.

This pocket garden is at the front of the house. We took out our side of the sidewalk, removed the stones and replaced the soil. It's only 16 feet long and 28 inches wide but it's possible to get dozens and dozens of plants in such a small space. From the left: *Tovara virginiana* 'Painter's Palette', which looks like a houseplant. It's very hardy and sits comfortably next to variegated *Lysimachia punctata* 'variegata' (no longer one of my favorites) and *Iris pallida,* which is positively unkillable. I've chopped this plant up and moved it all over the garden. The edgers are lavenders that have seeded themselves into the space along with the coralbells, *Heuchera*. This is how it looks in June or at least looked until I started moving things about.

Alliums are critical to all small gardens. They are elegant and slim and you can pop them in almost any place that suits your temperament. With a variety of these bulbs, you can have them blooming from spring to autumn. Above left: *Allium schoenoprasum* may be a very ordinary plant, but it is useful, tasty and beautiful. I've always had chives in this garden. Above right: *A. christophii*, or star-of-Persia, is a stunner. I leave the silvery flower heads to dry naturally in place. Then there is the ubiquitous *A.* 'Purple Sensation' (opposite), which makes a great statement when it's used by the dozen. Alliums, which should be planted in fall, require little care beyond giving them well-drained soil and sun. Another plus: squirrels won't touch them.

I dug a huge hole and filled it with gravel and sand, then piled up soil until it was almost a berm. In went the ornamental pear and on went a thick layer of mulch. It looked pathetic and did nothing except survive the winter. It put out silver leaves in a half-hearted way the following spring. This state persisted for four years. Then a few years ago, it decided to stay. It now has the most wonderful mantle of white blossoms in spring and has looked like a proper tree since then.

Alas, it was placed to balance a Russian olive, *Elaeagnus angustifolia*, on the opposite side of the garden and a sea buckthorn, *Hippophae rhamnoides*, on the other side of my neighbor's garden. The Russian olive is looking worse and worse by comparison, and I'm afraid that after decades of service, it's got to go. It will free up a large area where I can play some more, and I won't regret its passing one bit. Not that it isn't a good tree; I'm just tired of it, and I'll find something else to take its place. I think of the possibilities — *Styrax*, *Parrotia*, *Stewartia*, *Chionanthus*, and so on — and it makes me really excited. So much of the fun of gardening is in the making of plans.

There is nothing quite as striking as silver plants in containers: *Helichrysum petiolare* trailing to one side or *H. italicum* (syn. *H. angustifolium*), curry plant, which has a strong, spicy scent. Both are grace notes to be placed where they can be touched and smelled. I have brought the former through the winter by taking cuttings, but they are so cheap and easy to find, it is almost not worth the effort if space is at a premium (though anything I can get through the winter indoors is a form of triumph). *Ballota pseudodictamnus* is another good structural plant for a container. It has gray, felted leaves and pink blooms, but it's the foliage that's paramount. The same goes for another silver beauty, *Plectranthus argentatus*, a magnificent plant with blue blooms that will act as a foil for almost any other plant. Left by itself in a hot, sunny place, it will get enormous; stuck in a pot with pelargoniums or coleus, it will be an outstanding backgrounder.

Containers are the backbone of the summer garden. I started out with one or two and now have dozens. To be sensible, you should have only as many as you can easily store, but that's never seemed to stop me if I spot one I particularly like. I want pots in every possible medium spilling all over the place. And I want to move them around so that I can jam in a bit of color if one area becomes particularly dull.

For annuals in pots, I usually combine some good soil, some soilless potting mix and compost, and if I remember to do so, I'll give them a bit of manure tea on occasion. If I'm growing perennials in pots, I use proper soil and always a large (at least 14 to 18 inches across) container. All pots should be raised off the ground so that water won't gather in the bottom. Good drainage, as usual, is essential.

There are lots of great plants to go in pots: grasses of almost any sort, but especially *Hakonechloa macra* 'Aureola', which looks as though the wind is riffling through it. A spark for any dull corner, since it will

Top left: *Cypripedium reginae*, the exquisite showy lady's slipper, the native woodland orchid. Top right: The enchanting iris is *I. sibirica* 'Flight of Butterflies'. This is just one of many Siberian irises I have in the garden and it's aptly named. Lower left: The handsome balloon flower, *Platycodon grandiflorus*, starts with a balloon-like bud and then opens up into these bell-shaped flowers. It is in the same family as campanulas. Lower right: This is the white form of *Campanula persicifolia*, the peach-leaved bellflower. It also comes in blue and double forms. I rigorously pinch off the dying blooms and this one goes on for weeks.

grow in the shade. Hostas do very well in pots and will put up with a lot of neglect. I've had one in a plastic pot for several years. It sits in almost no light, and yet with the occasional watering, a bit of compost and manure tea, it, too, prospers.

Groundcovers allowed to go mad in a container will tumble about gracefully. A pot is the only place for something as vicious as variegated goutweed, *Aegopodium podagraria* 'Variegatum'. It's a good-looking plant but, alas, has roots that will penetrate anything alive. It's possible to keep it under control for years, and then it's off. Every time it's disturbed, the root system will split and become more vigorous.

Another plant that should be outlawed anywhere except in a pot is the plume poppy, *Macleaya cordata*, which has near-gray foliage and a large écru plume that comes out in August. It's very pleasing at first, then turns pugnacious in its desire to take over. It will grow to 8 feet tall in semishade and about 5 feet in deep shade, which is probably the only thing that slows it down. Confined to a pot, though, it makes a gracious statement.

The rampant artemisias, *A. ludoviciana* 'Silver King' and *A. l.* 'Silver Queen' and even *A. stelleriana* 'Silver Brocade', a groundcover with deeply notched leaves, will spill decoratively over the sides of containers; and *A. pontica*, ruinous in the garden, is charming when potted and clipped into a mounded shape. Lambs' ears, *Stachys byzantina*, is another good silver pot perennial. Any grass in the *Miscanthus sinensis* family should also be considered.

Echeverias are tender perennials, but they make superb container landscapes combined with sempervivums of every color, stripe and web. Along with other succulent plants, you can make a landscape design in miniature using one or two of these luscious things as a central focus.

Bringing silver and gold into the shady sections of the garden is another important principle of planting. Shade decorated by nothing but hostas and impatiens is boring. Mixing up various ferns, pulmonarias and lamiums will make a good display all summer. I particularly like *Lamium maculatum* 'White Nancy', a traditional and very useful form, *Pulmonaria saccharata* 'Sissinghurst White' and *P. s.* 'Mrs. Moon' (pink), all with nicely splotched silver leaves. *P. rubra* 'David Ward' has large whitish leaves with a pale green center. The blooms are a pinky orange, which might be difficult to combine with other colors, but the foliage alone is worth it. *P. longifolia* 'Bertram Anderson' has narrow, pointed leaves and intense blue blooms. This is a good family to explore, and new ones are coming into the trade all the time.

Campanulas are another group of plants I wouldn't be without. They really touch my heart. But they're a little like my wardrobe — I keep buying the same things over and over again. *Campanula glomerata* is beauteous, with extraordinary, large blue-purple bells. It grows 2 feet in the shade without any danger of falling over. I cannot praise this plant too much, and I swear every year I feel I must buy another one.

This group is right next to the deck and there are days when I would like to take a bath in its sensuality. A variegated elder, *Sambucus nigra*, is cut back each spring to keep its variegation as brilliant as this. The artemisia is *A.* x 'Huntington' and my favorite by a long shot. It's just about the hardiest one I've found, and the amount of growth it puts on in one season is truly staggering. The deep burgundy color belongs to *Sedum* 'Möhrchen', a plant whose tones get more and more intense as autumn approaches.

Containers are the moveable feast of the garden. They supply color in summer and make creative combinations. Opposite: The purple-green tones of *Eupatorium rugosum* 'Chocolate' make the perfect foil for the bright leaves of coleus. I don't recommend putting more than three of these plants together and they should be chosen very carefully. *Coleus* 'Inky Fingers' is in the foreground, supported by *C.* 'Red Ruffles' and *C.* 'Coral Glow' in the rear. Above left: This container combines *C.* 'Red Coat', with *C.* 'Betelgeuse' peeking out behind and, to my mind the best of all, the lime green coleus, *C.* 'The Line' which can be used with just about anything. Above right: That's *Lonicera nitida* 'Baggesen's Gold' in the rear with heliotrope and lobelia.

C. cochlearifolia is a traveling form but easy to pull out. It has decorative petite bells in blue or white. *C. garganica* grows to 4 inches and makes a carpet of purply-blue flowers. There are dozens more, and I'm always looking for a spot to tuck one into.

Lobelias were never high on my list of Most Desirable Plants. I have had *Lobelia* x *gerardii*, a slender blue bloom that will seed itself all over the place. I got fed up with pulling it out and was determined to acquire no more. Then I met the amazing hybrid *L.* x *speciosa* 'Rose Beacon' and put it in a spot where most plants are unwilling to grow — shady, damp in spring, dry in summer. In spite of this, it has turned into a most exquisite clump of brilliant rose blooms 3 feet tall, as happily ensconced as anything else.

There are other hybrid lobelias I like almost as well such as *L.* 'Gladys Lindley' (pure white) and *L.* 'Russian Princess' (a deep magenta). Lobelia is a plant that attracts bees, submits quite happily to deadheading and, in these named forms, doesn't spread itself around unwittingly. Just good solid clusters you can count on. And they work so well with other plants because of their upright way of growing.

Putting plants together is probably what got me started as an obsessive gardener. I remember looking at a garden book many years ago and thinking, I can do that, when I saw two plants that looked so perfect together they almost seemed like a painting. I set out then to find plants that would look good with each other. If you just think about color, of course, there's no trick to it at all. You get a color wheel going in your head and make pleasing combinations. But getting it absolutely right so that you've got the blooms coming out simultaneously and plants with exactly the same needs for light, soil and moisture to really thrive, then you've got the most magic moment in all of gardening.

Sometimes I like traditional, almost clichéd, associations such as Shasta daisies with *Rosa* 'The Fairy'. It was one of the first ones I figured out by myself. How could I know I'd eventually see it everywhere? And does that even matter? It pleases me. Because they looked so good together, I was moved to try another combination. Then another and another, until before I knew it, I had a border that looked electrifying. It was the breakthrough in my gardening. I was turning into a thoughtful kind of gardener, not just putting one plant after another — plonk, plonk, plonk.

Combinations go way beyond cultural affinities and color because shape and texture also play a big part in what actually looks good together. I've always loved lambs' ears alternating with woody thymes or skirting the bottom of tall hardy geraniums. There is a nonblooming lambs' ears with huge felted gray-green leaves called *Stachys byzantina* 'Countess Helene von Stein' that is even better than the species. In this case, the smooth quality of the geranium with the soft velvet of the stachys is a pleasure. Picking up tones from plant to plant is also a good guide for placement. Choose a shade in the leaf of a coralbell, for instance,

One of the most versatile container plants is any form of licorice plant, *Helichrysum petiolare*, which comes in tones of grey, yellow and combinations thereof. To the right of this silvery group is *Euphorbia dulcis* 'Chameleon', probably one of the most useful garden plants there is. It's like a mysterious shadow with its deep purple foliage. The leaves turn red and gold in autumn. The silver plant in the background is *Plectranthus argentatus*, which is a really important gray foliage plant for containers. It's easy to take cuttings and winter this one over. The sprinkling of little flowers in the foreground is *Calamintha nepeta*.

Lobelias are fascinating plants. We tend to think of the trailing lobelias (*L. erinus* cultivars) so beloved for containers. But there are clumping forms of tall perennial lobelias I wouldn't be without. Above left: *Lobelia x gerardii* is a strong blue. Above right: The hybrid, *L. x speciosa* 'Rose Beacon', is in a semi-shady spot, almost ignored, yet it fills out and makes a good show and I find it breathtaking. Opposite: *L.* 'Gladys Lindley' is such a pure white it lights up its corner of the border perfectly. The hybrids may not all be hardy but they are worth growing even for a single year. They like moist soil and shelter from very hot sun.

and then put it close to a plant that echoes the same color. *Heuchera americana* 'Eco-Magnififolia' next to *Euphorbia amygdaloides* 'Purpurea' does this for me. Each picks up the other's shades of green-into-purple. And then, just to add a fillip, I put them both in front of a *Kerria japonica* 'Picta', which in my experience, has none of the species' problems with size and disease. The pale variegation of the kerria acts as an ideal backdrop of lightness.

Another knockout combination is a purple avens, *Geum rivale*, given to me by a friend and then popped in alongside an *Enkianthus campanulatus*. This is a really good shrub with a slender, vase-like shape that will take the partial shade of this section of the garden. The enkianthus has bell-like pink flowers with a slightly darker edging that hang down gracefully. The edging is exactly the same shade as the avens with its upward-facing blossoms. Both come into bloom at the same time. This was a supreme example of serendipity.

Every garden needs lots of shrubs incorporated with perennials, annuals and bulbs. This type of mixed border is ideal for any northern gardener. In our climate, a completely herbaceous border looks awful in winter with nothing but nasty little stubs to account for its presence. It seems obvious to say "site a shrub properly right at the outset," but having broken this rule so often by constantly moving these poor things about, I can assure you, it takes them a long time to recover. When I look at the size of the shrubs in my garden, it's easy to tell which ones were moved several times before I was finally satisfied.

Never plant a cluster of the same shrubs close together. I find it an offence to see landscaping companies jam together three or four dogwoods such as *Cornus alba* 'Siberica' when each will want space to make a splash of bright red bark in winter. And never buy big shrubs, even if you want to have a good display immediately. The smaller, the better, so that they get time to acclimatize. With any size shrub, make sure it has lots and lots of time to get established during the growing season.

When planting around shrubs, it's important to give them enough room so that nothing is interfering with the root systems. I noticed this when I was planting bulbs and tucking them in under shrubs that wouldn't leaf out until later in the spring. Though the bulbs did just fine, the shrubs would sometimes languish, and now I don't put bulbs much closer than about a foot from the main stem (see Autumn).

You can't always choose neighbors, but if you are as lucky as I am, you'll find some who are cooperative and love plants too. On the south side of our fence, Diana and Bruce have two adorable little kids. And in a spirit of largesse, they installed a stone wall slightly more than halfway back to keep their kids contained and left me to plant the remainder.

Nothing could warm a greedy gardener's heart more than to be allowed additional space. Down came the horrible metal fence separating us at the back and in went a new berm assembled from the bits

Here is the back of the garden viewed through the redbud, *Cercis canadensis* 'Forest Pansy', whose leaves get to a more and more intense purple over the season. To the right is Clethralnifolia, which blooms in mid-summer. It is surrounded by small golden hostas and a variety of pulmonarias.

of wood left from taking out an old tree. The pile was topped with soil and manure, and it has been slowly, very slowly, composting down these seven years. This echoes the berm on my side, so there's more contouring back here all at the same level. I covered their berm with divisions of hostas, sedums and grasses from my own garden, and a wonderful peony that's probably been in this garden for 80 years found a new and satisfactorily dramatic site.

This became the new Jardin des Refusés — not that these are plants I've refused, but the plants I don't quite know what to do with. This is a luxury every gardener should have: a place for a great deal of mind-changing. In this area, I've put in lots of native plants such as black-eyed Susan (*Rudbeckia fulgida*), meadowsweet (*Filipendula rubra*) and the delicious pink lady's slipper (*Cypripedium acaule*). I've also put in a purple birch to give it a central focus. We moved in a red-leafed rose, a sea buckthorn and an old forsythia to give it an all-season background.

There are big plants, too, that I can no longer accommodate on my side: a monstrous cow parsnip (*Heracleum*), *Darmera peltata* and *Petasites japonicus*. The last two, both lush, water-loving plants, used to sit supreme on my berm. Now the darmera has pretty much gone (it's just too vigorous for a small space) and the petasites is constantly being pulled out. I leave just enough for it to act as an indicator plant. This part of the garden has an unusually high water table (the underground pond and stream), so if the petasites starts wilting and falling over, that means things are desperate and everything needs some water. I used to have an underground water system that I was always digging up because the black tubing looked exactly like a truculent root. I finally got fed up and reverted to having spigots with hoses in three different places through the garden.

I prefer hand-watering to anything else. I like to hunker down with a hose running slowly in any part of the garden that seems to need this attention. I water very deeply and usually without a sprinkler. More recently, I've had a water barrel installed to capture rainwater and save it from going straight down the drain. This is a wonderful thing with a tap that makes it easy to fill big watering cans.

This would be impossible in a huge garden, but the principle is important if not the method. It's astonishing to dig into the soil and find that the top 4 inches seem moist enough but that it's dead dry below that. It explains why many plants simply give up. They need to have water at the bottom of their root systems to grow well, not at the top. One more important reason to mulch is that it lets the water filter down through the upper layers in a natural way rather than pounding the soil with a direct torrent. It's no trouble to let a hose sit in place for an hour to slowly water a large tree or shrub. And it is much better for the plants.

This shot of the Jardin des Refusés has my very first combination: Shasta daisies with the ever-blooming shrub rose, *Rosa* 'The Fairy'. I cut the daisy back to each new bit of growth and nip off the dead roses. This is one of the places where I like to sit for the early morning sun and just inhale the whole garden. This area is beginning to look more and more like a formal little garden. I like doing things in pockets like this and changing them radically every few years.

Early in my gardening life, I wanted an arbor and a potting bench. I also wanted a waterfall, a pond, a gazebo and a bridge and a lot of sun. But you can't have everything in one garden. Never, ever install something you don't admire. There's no such thing as temporary in gardening. Once something important has been set in place, plants grow all around, you get used to it and it's there forever.

Thus the arbor. A bit of a joke between me and the carpenter. Just stick one in, and I'll get a proper one later, said I. Fifteen years on, it's still there and to actually get rid of it and replace it with something better will cost a fortune. I should have spent the money in the first place. Gardening seems to be one long lesson in sensible actions. You have to mature into gardening.

The potting bench was another total bust. I seldom potted things and, when I did, it was on the table on the back deck. The potting bench became a repository for all manner of junk. A walk through the garden was a walk past an eyesore.

As these things happen, along came someone with enough imagination to change it. The potting bench evolved into a two-hole compost bin with a removable front disguised by swinging gates of square lattice. I can take the boards out and turn the compost easily myself. I got rid of one of those plastic things that take way too long and don't allow the compost to breathe. An L-shaped, square lattice screen on two sides of the large compost bins creates a well-disguised work area in the middle of the garden. It's convenient and a good place to store all the bags of compost, manure, coco-fiber and plastic pots.

Everything is recycled in this garden. The kitchen parings come here, as do all the nonseedy weeds and green plant cuttings. I can't cope with the bigger woody stuff, so that goes into the city recycling. My method of composting is utterly simple: a layer of leaves on the bottom, then green/brown layers until the top of the pile is complete. (Green = kitchen cuttings; brown = leaves.) To heat up and attract the right kind of worms (red wigglers), a compost heap needs to be a minimum of 3 feet by 3 feet by 3 feet, or 1 cubic yard. Two cubic yards (roughly 4 by 4 by 3 feet) is preferable. I wait until I can feel the heat, let it be for a couple of days, then start turning things over.

This is relaxing and stretches my upper body muscles. I'm also fascinated by the extraordinary amount of life in the compost. To work the compost is to stare into the face of a lot of things crawling about. There is nothing but a good sweet smell from here, and it always astonishes me when people don't want to put their hands into this great stuff. Within about six weeks, it's finished enough to mix with ground-up leaves, coco-fiber and manure to make an excellent mulch. It's then dispersed around the garden wherever it's needed to protect soil from weeds and to keep in moisture. It will continue to break down and feed plants as they require it.

This is the view from the berm back to the bower. The grasses in the foreground have to live through floods and drought on an annual basis. *Phalaris arundinacea* 'Feesey's Form' is whiter and less aggressive than the ordinary ribbon grass or gardener's garters as it's known. Behind is *Alopecurus pratensis* 'Aureus', a grass which also thrives in extreme conditions.

The need for clematis in all three seasons is never more apparent than when you see them lined up. I tend to plant them about 2 or 3 feet from each other along fences and they get tangled up. It's the flow of color I'm interested in even if growing them this way makes it more difficult to prune. Above left: This double flower is *C.* 'Vyvyan Pennell'. It was an early choice and is much fluffier than any I would choose now. Above right: *C.* 'Gipsy Queen' is a lovely purple form.

I prefer simpler forms such as above left *C.* 'Rouge Cardinal' with *C.* x *jackmanii.* I cut the latter back severely in spring when the first buds erupt. Above right: *C. alpina* 'Ruby' comes out in spring. These are all along one stretch of fence and, with sweet autumn clematis, *C. terniflora,* I've got color from early to late in the growing season.

There are much fancier ways of composting and mulching, but this simple method works just fine for me. The only thing I never have enough of is leaves. I had to give up stealing my neighbors' leaves when they began recycling. For a while, I'd get my husband to drive through other parts of town, piling bags in the back of the car, but he found it just too embarrassing. Now I depend on the kindness of friends with country gardens and small forests.

A work station may be an essential garden ingredient, but so is storage. I have a small shed at the side of the house where I put pots in winter and what little equipment I use. I have a work station where I can make soil mixtures for containers and put together mulch. I have my storage shed. So why is my deck always cluttered with all this stuff? Because it's easy. My lack of housekeeping shows up glaringly there, and to receive guests means a lot of work cleaning up. I know I'm never going to change this habit because I garden alone for the most part, and I garden for me.

The garden in high summer really struts its stuff with this lush quantity of color and greenery. I love the sound of summer when the garden is alive with birds and insects. To the left, there is a butterfly bush, *Buddleia* 'Lochinch', one of the toughest I've found. Butterflies are really attracted to its deep violet-blue flowers. Elsewhere, the huge, umbrella-shaped flower heads of eupatorium are a magnet for bees. To me, the waves of color in the garden seen from the cool shade of the deck are heartstopping in their beauty. The coleus in containers frame the scene, and even the beastly weeping willow looks good at this time of year.

- Pinch off the leaf of a plant. If it has a scent, it's a herb.
- Herbs need four hours of sun a day to survive.
  They like nutrient-poor soil, but rich soil will produce giants.
- To change soil for herbs, dig a hole, add up to 80 percent 3/4" gravel and 20 percent
  garden soil. This works for any plant that needs sharp drainage and thin soil.
- Use a stone mulch as a good background for plants. Pebbles or crushed stone will look
  good and provide both warmth and nutrients.
- Don't overfeed plants. In nature, plants are tighter and more beautiful in form
  than our fleshy, over-pampered garden varieties.
- Don't run grass right up to the base of trees; keep other plants at a distance.
- Pruning: Some woody plants are best pruned in summer because they bleed too
  much in spring. These include maple, birch, hickory, honey locust, linden, magnolia,
  poplar, Virginia creeper, Boston ivy and grape. Prune out dead or diseased branches,
  then prune for form, taking out useless side branches, layers with no meaning to the
  overall shape. The best way is to lie down under the tree or shrub and look up to
  see what it needs. This was good enough for Russell Page.
- Cut back climbing hydrangea, *Hydrangea petiolaris*, after it's finished blooming
  to keep it from becoming blowsy.
- Annuals for containers: *Plectranthus purpuratus*, *P. argentatus*, *Bidens ferulifolia*,
  multiflora *Petunia*, *Nicotiana langsdorffii*, *Cerinthe major*, *Hypericum* x *moserianum*
  'Tricolor'. (I've tried this in borders. It isn't comfortable, and is definitely not hardy.)
- Plant containers right up to the end of summer. This is not transplanting; it's transferring
  from one container to another.
- If you don't mulch, use plants that are hardy to a zone colder than the one you're
  living in (in zone 6, use zone 5 plants).
- *Anthriscus sylvestris* 'Ravenswing' is a burgundy foliage plant that I like very much.
  It looks a bit like Queen Anne's lace but with lovely dark foliage. It will seed about
  but looks good even in the shade. *Cryptotaenia japonica* is another burgundy
  shade plant with the same habit, and I love it.

summer tips

stars of summer

Alliums
Artemisias
Campanulas
Clematis
Coralbells
Hakonechloa macra 'Aureola'
Hybrid lobelias
Red-leafed rose
Schizophragma hydrangeoides
Thalictrum
Weeping silver pear

autumn

There are brief moments approaching the autumn shoulder when the garden reaches a new level of perfection.

The plants have a burnished quality, and the crystalline light sharpens each detail. It is breathtaking, with an almost elegiac quality that touches me deeply. I wait in anticipation for the dazzling colors that will soon be part of my view.

Autumn is close to my heart. We bought our house in September of 1967. I was so amazed at actually owning property, and so much of it, that I wasn't quite sure where to start. I wanted to possess this place, to make it beautiful. So that first year, we took out bags and bags of neglect — weeds massive in size and quantity. Eventually, I could also see that someone had planted before me. I recognized a classic peony and a vast accumulation of self-seeding pink cosmos.

It was almost as though this garden was designed for autumn, since that's when I began to garden in earnest. I decided almost immediately, in spite of the debris, that I needed daisies. I searched everywhere until I found a leftover pot of tatty Shastas at a local garden center and popped them in the ground. Quite the gardener, I thought. I've made my mark.

To the neophyte, everything that grows is sacred. While I yanked out weeds by the barrowload, at the same time, I could hardly bear to pull out thistles because they looked so good in bloom. And I left untouched ox-eye daisies, Queen Anne's lace and goldenrod without realizing what good choices they were for a healthy garden.

I think I picked up my passion for ecological gardening when I was writing magazine stories on the environment back in the 1960s as alarm bells began to sound about how we were turning our planet toxic. Rachel Carson had made a enormous impression on me. And it certainly would never have occurred to me to use herbicides to get rid of weeds once I'd read the list of contents on a weed-and-feed bag. It was enough to convince me that I didn't want this stuff around my kids and cat. I knew absolutely nothing about plant diseases. I recognized slugs but had never heard of an earwig or any of the multitude of other bugs that might like to live here.

The so-called weeds I left were habitat for all sorts of good creatures such as ladybugs, which consume bad bugs such as aphids. I had read about that. I also knew enough about ecology to realize that if I had a generous mix of plants in my garden, they would probably look after themselves. It was the second autumn that I put in a serviceberry (*Amelanchier canadensis*), a purple-leaf sand cherry, a weeping mulberry, a red-twig dogwood and a birch tree. This started a habit of installing major plants in the autumn. My reasoning was that there was time for root systems to take hold before hard frost and plants were usually on sale. I suspect that the latter was the greater part of the equation, money being in very short supply then. The prevalent attitude at the time was that gardening wasn't a very serious pastime and you certainly didn't put a lot of

The serviceberry, *Amelanchier canadensis*, is one of the backbones of the whole garden. In autumn, the leaves hold this glorious color for weeks. The birds flit in to pick off the few remaining berries. To the left is silverleaf dogwood, *Cornus alba* 'Elegantissima', another super-hardy plant that lights up a gloomy section of the woodland berm. The shrub in the foreground is the perky star magnolia, *Magnolia stellata*, which will eventually be the focal point of this area. Behind it is a variegated nannyberry, *Viburnum lentago* 'Variegata'. The textured surround of hostas, ferns and grasses make this a vibrant area.

money into it. But the instinct for autumnal planting was bang on, it turns out, not just for woody plants but for perennials as well.

It was an autumn many years later when Laurie and Robert, our neighbors to the north, and I decided we should do something radical about the fence between our properties. We spent the summer having a new fence built of wide, 4-inch-square lattice. Though it looked so much better than the dull, brown slab that had preceded it, we also decided it should go only a third of the way down the garden. From there on, we'd have a line of shrubs that would be a hedgerow in the old-fashioned sense, a living fence. We kept the posts running at regular intervals to the very back of the garden just in case this idea didn't work out. Friendly as we are, we weren't about to take chances. The spaces in between the posts were woven with a barrier of heavy-duty fishing line. We watched as their dog leapt for joy right into this invisible wire. The memory of that pranging would stay forever. I have never had a problem with their dog coming into my garden, even though the fishing wire fell down years ago.

Laurie and Robert said, "You choose the plants, we'll split the cost." It was sheer pleasure doing the research, finding the pictures of what each one would look like. There were a number of factors at work, but the most important one in choosing plants was the differing light conditions down the row.

I planted vines along our mutual fence almost immediately. There was a nonflowering wisteria close to the house that was already old when we started the project, but I then planted bittersweet, *Celastrus scandens*. This is absolutely the wrong vine for any garden, certainly a small garden, and it took about eight years for that to become woefully apparent. Oh, it looks good, especially when the burnt-orange seeds burst open to expose the jewel-like amber interior. Laurie and I like to cut lengths for our Thanksgiving tables. But it's way too vigorous for this space. It pops up all over the place, and my only recourse is to whack it back severely every year to keep it down to 30 feet. In many areas, it is banned because it is so invasive.

I added other, much more agreeable vines: *Clematis* x *jackmanii*, *C. alpina* 'Ruby', *C. texensis*, *C. maximowicziana* (as it was in those days; now it's *C. terniflora*), *C.* 'Duchess of Edinburgh' and a lovely variegated porcelain vine, *Ampelopsis brevipedunculata* 'Elegans'. Its small pink-and-white mottled leaves tucked in behind a couple of clematis and through the bittersweet look enchanting. The cobalt-blue berries make autumn a time of grace. It will seed about — this is another plant that can get out of hand in the wrong situation. Be careful when you are planting any kind of nonnative plant to make sure that in your area it isn't invasive and can't cause any damage. These occupied the wall of the first room of the garden.

Starting in the second room, in the shade, came our mutual shrubs: *Acanthopanax sieboldianus*; *Cornus alternifolia*; *Hamamelis* x *intermedia* 'Ruby Glow', which usually blooms in February; *Viburnum* x

Japanese maples, *Acer palmatum*, can make a strong impact in a small garden. Just never encase them in grass or leave them to grow all by themselves. They like company and should be placed with care because of their strong autumn hues. Clockwise from top left: Coralbark maple, *A.p.* 'Sango-kaku'; *A.p.* 'Scolopendrifolium'; *A.p.* 'Dissectum Atropurpureum, the first Japanese maple to come into the garden; *A.p.* 'Shindeshojo', the most recent arrival. Avoid exposing these plants to blazing noonday sun or they'll bleach out. Protection from the southern sun in winter is also advisable to prevent frost-cracking.

pragense, a plant that stays evergreen all winter; *V.* x *juddii*, with divinely scented spring blooms; and a variegated dogwood that looks so right, I'm still struck by the perfection of its placement. There's enough room for its wide, branching form, and in summer, its silver-edged leaves make this corner luminescent.

Not everything was so successful in such consistent shade. *Shepherdia*, a felted gray shrub that supposedly loves shade, languished for years before I moved it out of its misery. Then there was the stephanandra. This was where my lack of experience showed up. There are several forms of stephanandra. I thought I was getting *Stephanandra incisa,* which would have been perfect with an arching shape about 10 feet tall. The one I got was a good groundcovering shrub for shade, *S. i.* 'Crispa', and not the stand-up shrub we needed. It was ridiculous in the location. I ignored the information on the label and should have placed it elsewhere or sent it back. It is foolish to disregard labels and the research they present. Another factor is that no matter how hard you try to be accurate, the varying soil and light conditions will make every plant behave at a slight variance with whatever books or labels say. Only experience and time can provide this information.

Another error was to include *Sorbaria sorbifolia.* I like this plant. The cut leaves are pleasing and so are the nodding white plumes. But it spreads willy-nilly all over the place. I wish, in this case, the tag had stated: Do Not Plant This Unless You Have a Large Country Property, or some such caveat. It's hard for neophytes to understand things like a plant becoming rampant until they've endured it in their own gardens.

Other things, alas, croaked, and I'm not quite sure why: *Cornus kousa*, the lovely Japanese dogwood meant as a focal point; a deutzia; and a beautyberry, *Callicarpa bodnieri* var. *giraldii* 'Profusion', with gorgeous turquoise seeds. I tried beautyberry in other parts of the garden, but none have taken, so I've given up for the moment. I believe that even in the sunniest parts of my garden, there isn't enough for this plant.

In the back third of the garden in the Jardin des Refusés, things were shaping up when I planted ornamental grasses. *Miscanthus sinensis* 'Variegatus' reigns beside what was supposed to be a golden form of elder but is plain old *Sambucus canadensis*. We were victims of false labeling here. I don't care, because it is the most profuse producer of fruit I've ever seen and the birds love it. Flocks of them take turns waiting to get at the deep black berries, and it's a wonderful sight, this cooperation. Then there's a lovely little katsura tree that down the road may get too big for its position but is very nice at the moment.

One of my triumphs comes next: a yellow *Rosa hugonis* and *Viburnum plicatum tomentosum* 'Shasta' with dozens of purple alliums planted nearby. Most years, they bloom together in what can only be described as heart-stopping beauty. More recently, a yellow-flowering magnolia has been added to the mix. It defines what spring should look like to me.

Altogether, our fence has worked out extremely well. The shrubs have taken over where the wooden fence ended, and we, at least, are not aware of the posts at all. It's easy enough for us to crawl through it to

This is the overview of the back garden from the third-floor deck. I like to dash upstairs to figure out what I should be moving around and where new things must be put in. The overall feeling that I'm hoping to create is a dense tapestry of color and texture. This shows how structured the garden really is rather than the loose, ephemeral look it has at ground level. It's important to look at your garden from every vantage point in the house, as well as the roof. You get an extremely interesting perspective on garden design. Taking photographs in black and white will also reveal any structural flaws.

visit or to chop back the vines on their side, and the dog doesn't bother to explore on my side. In very recent years, Laurie has also installed a berm to echo the shape of my own and filled it with native plants. This gives the illusion of both gardens being much larger than they actually are. And we get the pleasure of each other's work.

Planting that many shrubs and trees at one go gave me a great deal of insight into what woody plants need to survive. Autumn is the ideal time of year to get these plants into the ground if there are at least six weeks of frost-free weather ahead. The soil is still warm, and the potential for retaining oxygen is at its highest, encouraging root growth.

It used to be common wisdom that it was important to dig a deep hole. But that's been pretty much contradicted over the past few years. There's a conventional notion that roots mirror the tops of trees and shrubs and stop at the drip line. In reality, they spread out three or four times farther. From these main roots reaching outward are little feeder roots, which run from 3 to 6 inches below the surface. Most roots run laterally, as anyone dealing with a silver or Norway maple can attest. But it's also true for all other trees, including oaks with their legendary deep tap roots. Most roots want to stay in that top bit of soil, where humus is adding nutrients to the soil.

It's best to dig a hole that's no deeper than the root system but about five times the width of the container or root ball. Then backfill with the same soil and tamp it down level with the ground. For years, I mixed compost or sheep manure in with the soil, thinking I was doing the plant a big favor. But down the road, the roots will be reluctant to grow beyond the good stuff, and the tree or shrub can go into serious shock. So now I use the soil from the hole as is. The important thing is to add a 3-to-4-inch-deep layer of mulch and make sure the plant has enough water in the first year. Most plants don't need to be mollycoddled. Survival is the name of the game, in gardening as in nature.

As usual, there should be good drainage and the right soil for the plant. If you want to put an acid-loving plant into clay, you'll have to amend such a huge area it's not worth the effort. Either get another plant or expect that it will remain very, very small, as my own efforts have proved.

Autumn is also the best time of year to construct new beds. This is when we ripped up the front garden, which had looked pathetic for years in the shadow of a giant silver maple. There was nothing much to recommend the area; few things grew here. I added loads of manure and planted myrtle, *Vinca minor*. Nothing. I tried sod. Even creeping Jenny wouldn't take. I didn't realize the ground was so compacted from months of having construction equipment sitting on it that it would take years before the soil could support more than the tree. But it dawned, albeit slowly, that the whole area would have to change if there was to be a front garden at all.

In a flash of brilliance, I decided on raised beds as being the only way it was possible to garden under such a giant forest tree and in such terrible soil. I had edges built and filled with yards and yards of good triple

Right: *Artemisia lactiflora* is a froth of white in front of a eupatorium. I put really tall plants together so they can lean on each other. Any sedum is a good autumn plant but *Sedum* 'Möhrchen' (left) is so strong-willed, it's a must for just about any garden. Sedums match up happily with almost all forms of aster.

mix. I also had my son Chris dig in bags of leaves, and then I just let it sit over the winter. By spring, I had almost friable soil untouched by weeds and pretty much ready for planting. We had done the same thing in the Jardin des Refusés when the tarmac was pulled up, but it took three years to revive the soil there because it was so completely dead. Be warned if you are trying this that those maple roots will be very happy to reinvade. It's a battle between plants and tree. Compost and manure will probably keep everybody happy.

Though it's a fairly shady spot, I decided to go for edgers of lavenders. (The one that survived to look the best was *Lavandula angustifolia* 'Hidcote Blue'.) They make sculptural forms beneath the snow with their clean, distinctive shapes and stay presentable when all else is appearing desperate in autumn. Over the years, they've flopped over the wooden edges, softening them. The lavenders were interspersed with woody thymes such as *Thymus* x *citriodorus* (a lemon-scented species) and *T.* x *c.* 'Bertram Anderson' (a golden form), as well as lambs' ears, *Stachys byzantina*. Behind them were pink Asiatic lilies and several shrubs, including *Spiraea japonica* 'Anthony Waterer' (also listed as *S.* x *bumalda*).

Far be it from me to knock any plant, but that spirea has been moved at least four times because I just can't seem to get it right. This is partly, I think, because it's so overused in public places that I'm now weary of it. It did end up in a great place in the front garden once I discovered that severe cutting-back (coppicing) will keep a dull plant like this looking young and fresh. And I'm talking about cutting it back to a mere 3 or 4 inches from the ground. If this is done every year, the plant won't get blowsy.

Bridalwreath spirea, another ubiquitous shrub in our city, can also use a regular chopping-back. Unfortunately, these two plants are usually grown by those who think this treatment is an insult, so the plants just get bigger and droopier and, except for their brief, glorious bloom, look quite drab. If you don't coppice every year, then you should at least take out about a third of the stems at ground level to keep the inside full of light.

It's an uphill fight gardening under a silver maple, but now I'm feeding not only the tree but also hostas of varying kinds; a pretty arctic willow (*Salix purpurea* 'Nana'); a golden privet (*Ligustrum* 'Vicaryi'); *Viburnum farreri* 'Nanum'; *V. plicatum* 'Summer Snowflake'; *Itea virginica* 'Henry's Garnet', a great addition because of its magnificent autumn color; and dwarf lilac (*Syringa velutina*) — there are two of these, one close to the house because the scent is heavenly on these small shrubs. Bayberry, *Myrica pensylvanica*, is another excellent shrub that stays green part of the winter. I have to remember, however, that this is probably the last one to leaf out in spring and to neither panic nor prune.

For many years, the border against the front porch was the pits. I hate most foundation plantings, especially those beloved by nurseries: one pointy evergreen, two rounded ones and a forsythia to complete the mix. But I didn't think my solution was much better. I had nepetas and phloxes, asters and

This view looking back toward the house in autumn shows the scrims of foliage that make up the layers of the garden. I like mounds of sensuality. Still looking fresh are the artemisias, *A.* 'Lambrook Silver' in the centre and *A.* x 'Huntington' in the background. Behind the lady is a white Japanese-flowered peony, *Paeonia lactiflora*, which is going to be way too big for its site. This is, after all, a garden in motion, but good siting in the first place would have been a much better idea.

chrysanthemums flopping over from lack of light and poor soil. Again, this was the neophyte. I didn't realize that the soil here would have to be dug out and replaced as well. Soil was dirt in those days, not the vibrant, living organism it is to me now.

The light conditions had also changed over the years, and only the dwarf lilac and a climbing hydrangea looked even vaguely respectable. The latter threatens to chew up the entire front porch. This is a complex plant, partly because it is such a good one. It will grow in the shade, clings on its own and has lovely lacecap flowers. Though it takes an age (five years, perhaps) to really take off, it can get out of control. It requires a good whacking-back after the blooms have passed. *Schizophragma hydrangeoides*, which I have in several spots in the back garden, would have been a far better choice. It has the lovely blooms but isn't nearly as assertive as climbing hydrangea.

At bulb-planting time during a recent autumn, I decided this 3-by-10-foot front border had to be renovated. I left the climbing hydrangea and the lilac, and out came a revolting gold euonymus, a dusty old hosta and all the pathetic perennials, plus the sweet woodruff, *Galium odoratum*, which was one of the few things that did well here. I dug down 8 inches and removed everything I could. Once again, I was astounded that any plant grew here at all, given the construction muck. It always staggers me how much plants want to exist and how much they will tell us if we let them. In went a mass of decent soil topped off with a mix of compost and coco-fiber.

I decided on an edging of new coralbells, *Heuchera*, which are among the most versatile of all the recent hybrids on the market. I planted *H.* 'Stormy Seas', 'Pewter Veil', 'Chocolate Ruffles' and 'Eco-Magnififolia'. The leaves of these remarkable plants will hold their green and/or purple splendor all winter long. I then planted a glossy Hicks yew, *Taxus* x *media* 'Hicksii'. And grabbed a compact inkberry, *Ilex glabra* 'Compacta', the moment I saw it in the nursery. It stays evergreen with a mass of shiny dark green leaves and small black berries. These plants looked great together year-round. The whole bed was underplanted with *Narcissus* 'Thalia' and *Muscari* backed by *Tulipa* 'Queen of Night'. I was thrilled with the effect.

This good solution was messed up when we decided that air-conditioning had to go in. There was absolutely no other place to put the wretched machine except right where the yew lived. It was moved to a sidewalk pocket garden and looks better there than it ever did up against the teal green of the house. I am now planning ways to disguise the air-conditioning unit — perhaps a small hedge of boxwood or a vine-covered screen. I hate having to deal with this kind of thing, but such are the realities of urban gardening. Of course, this would alter the whole front garden so radically that everything would have to be changed. This is how the gardening brain operates: one thing leads to another, usually with necessity pushing it all along.

The caption on page 102 should read:
Autumn leaves, of course, are what this season is all about. Throughout the growing season, the chlorophyll in the leaves masks the colors behind. But as the hours of sunlight are reduced, the underlying colors are revealed. Clockwise from top left: *Mahonia aquifolium* goes from this shiny green to a deep burgundy in the middle of winter; in spring it looks sad and then comes back from the center of the plant in acid green tones. The leaves of most hostas turn this gorgeous gold which always looks incredible with ferns. Lower right is a great little evergreen called *Juniperus communis* 'Gold cone'. The dwarf *Fothergilla gardenii* goes on for weeks in this dishy color. A North American native related to witch hazel, it likes a moist, acid soil. *Errata*

Necessity in my case frequently means getting fed up. One autumn a few years ago, I decided I couldn't get through another winter in darkness. I needed lights in the garden. This was for decoration more than safety, enhancement more than usefulness. I wanted to be able to sit in the gloom of the house and look at the garden lit up like a sculpture under the snow.

In this little garden, there was nothing major — no swimming pool or large statuary — that would be normal to light up. So I consulted the only lighting designer I knew, one experienced in stage and museum lighting. This turned into one of those wonderful learning experiences the garden constantly presents us with. And of course the work has to be started at night. What will this shrub look like glowing in the blackness of night? What will happen if that one is lit up instead? Lighting plants is simple compared with lighting moving actors, but he transferred something from the stage to the garden — a focus technique of highlighting individuals.

In my garden, where there are just a lot of plants, we needed to light for plant shapes rather than color and to give the plants form at night. The focus technique provides a feeling of space between the plants. When everything's lit up uniformly, you can't really appreciate one thing more than any other. The designer called what he was doing accidental lighting, or at least the feeling of accidental lighting, which focuses the attention on something important. And he wanted to keep that sense of moving from one room to another. Because he placed them so perfectly, we needed only six lights.

There are some things to consider about lighting: Don't put lights where they have a glare factor or shine in people's eyes; don't place them so that they bother neighbors; in a small space, don't light up both fences, since that makes them appear to come closer together. Good lighting is the lighting you don't notice. It should add just that right touch of magic.

The Japanese maple in the center of the checkerboard was a natural one to light from below to show off its fountain-like shape. The birch in the middle and another tree at the very back fence concentrated light on the central axis of the garden. Off to one side in each section, other plants were lit up. The red-leafed rose close to the house on the north side and the coralbark maple on the other were picked out, as were the small seating area near the center and the serviceberry. Thus, the eye is drawn to the very back, where the garden drifts off into a mysterious darkness. This is an investment I've enjoyed hugely ever since. I only light up the garden when we can sit and appreciate it, and what seemed like an extravagance at the outset has more than paid its way in pleasure.

I'm wild about autumn plants, and this is a wonderful time of year for plants to really show their stuff. It's the time when I get out my notebooks and put down the names of anything that looks dull for potential

The garden is full of rich colors once the cold weather starts moving in. The tall plant in the lower right is a hibiscus still in its pot waiting to be planted. I always look around for bargains and anything special, since autumn is one of the best times for planting if there's at least six weeks before hard frost. To the right are the white blooms of *Phlox paniculata* 'Mt. Fuji'. In the foreground is *Chelone obliqua*, the pink form of turtle-head. I deadhead obsessively and it lasts for weeks. So does the froth of white flowers from *Boltonia aster-oides*. This is a plant that should be pinched back somewhat in July to keep it from falling over.

Above left: Now, here's a combination I adore: *Salvia guaranitica* 'Purple Majesty' with *Solidago* 'Golden Wings', one of the newer forms of goldenrod, as a perfect foil. The salvia isn't hardy in my area but I don't care. I'll take it as an annual because it's just so gorgeous. Above right: *Aster novae-angliae* 'Harrington's Pink' seen in close-up. The large shot (right) shows it *in situ* behind the silvery artemisia, *A.* x 'Huntington'. This huge aster and the white-flowering *Boltonia asteroides* support each other gracefully and will cascade for weeks.

elimination because there's so much that's good. There are all the great and glorious asters and chrysanthemums, but I particularly like plants such as mint shrub, *Elsholtzia stauntonii*. It grows to about 5 feet and has a pleasant vase-like shape, and now it has gorgeous pinky-lilac spikes. In spring, it will be surrounded by *Narcissus* 'Petrel', a stunning small white daffodil.

One plant that I've come to love over all others in autumn is *Angelica gigas*. With magenta-to-crimson umbels (umbrella-like flower heads) and bronze foliage, it grows in sun or shade to over 3 feet tall in moist soil. I'm particularly fond of any form of bugbane, or snakeroot (*Cimicifuga*). Now this is a case where a plant gets its name changed when botanists reclassify the plant. It's now in the genus *Actaea*. Whether you buy it as *Actaea racemosa* or *Cimicifuga racemosa*, you have a splendid shade plant that requires only relatively moist soil with lots of humus to flourish. There are purple-leafed forms such as *C. simplex* 'Brunette' that are like fascinating shadows placed among other statuesque plants. A recent acquisition called 'Hillside Black Beauty' is a stunner. It will stay a deep burgundy even in shade, but don't get it too close to other plants. If its leaves are covered, they will revert to green. The cimicifuga part of the family will bloom anytime from late August right up to October.

The distinctive flowers of all forms of *Actaea* look like shooting stars at the ends of long, stiff stalks. Some of them will self-seed, and most of them are easy to divide in spring. There is a native form called doll's eyes, *A. pachypoda* (syn. *A. alba*), which has white fruit with a purple stigma, or "eye," that I find completely charming in the woodland in spring.

I mentioned the boltonia, which is a froth of flowers in autumn, but the eupatoriums are also good value — for example, *E. maculatum* 'Atropurpureum' with my favorite grass, Northern sea oats, *Chasmanthium latifolium*. This has flat, sculptural seedheads that will reveal themselves fully when the boltonia has to be cut back. *Panicum virgatum* 'Heavy Metal' is a grass with great dignity whose dark blue stalks rise to 4 feet. In fall it comes into its own undaunted by wind and rain.

Goldenrod, *Solidago*, gets a bad rap, and I've acquired several new forms that I think are going to prove to be great garden plants. You don't want to get rid of all the ones that seem to find their way unbidden into the garden, just keep them under control and don't let them go to seed. Don't ever fall for the claptrap that it contributes to allergies — that's ragweed. I never know where the goldenrod's pretty yellow heads will pop up, but usually it has the sense to be near a tall pink or purple aster or among the waning grace of a hosta.

Brunnera macrophylla 'Variegata' has blue flowers in spring but continues to look dramatic in autumn as long as it gets plenty of moisture. It has much larger heart-shaped leaves than the normal brunnera, with a wide cream brim. Another, called *B. m.* 'Langtrees', has subtle dots of silver about its large leaves.

Late autumn brings its own pleasures. Clockwise from top left: The blooms of *Viburnum plicatum* 'Summer Snowflake' do go on for months. Be careful siting this plant. It's often sold as a small shrub but it will get to at least 6 feet. *Caryopteris* x *clandonensis* is a hard-working plant that has silver foliage through three seasons and then comes out with this lovely flower. Toad lilies, *Tricyrtis*, are magnificent and they will get to be a fairly large stand in the proper woodland shade with moist, humusy soil. *T. hirta* var. *alba* and *T. formosana* (with a speckled orchid look) are just two of the more spectacular and showy forms of this plant.

One strange beauty, *Tovara virginiana* 'Painter's Palette', has the weirdest minuscule bright red blooms along slender stalks which poke up from highly decorative green leaves streaked with cream, pink and brown. This thing looks like a houseplant, and a friend once said, "Just one color too many, dear." But I don't care, I like it precisely for its bizarre appearance.

Autumn crocus, *Colchicum autumnale*, explodes in places where I'd completely forgotten I'd stuck it. The autumn crocus is one of the oldest plants in cultivation. There are so many now, it's possible to get a small collection going. Colors range from the palest mauve to flaming pinks. What a lift for the spirits. You buy them in fall, they bloom the first year and then disappear until the following autumn. Just try and remember where you planted them.

One year, I put in *Cryptotaenia japonica*, which isn't as fierce as it sounds. It's an elegant herb decked in dark purple, almost black leaves with dainty pink-white flowers. It thrives in deep shade. It seeds about in such a determined way that the first year, I couldn't figure out what was this new groundcover I had. Well, it was *Cryptotaenia* (or kryptonite), and it was everywhere. No matter, it pulls out easily enough, manages to look good wherever I let it stay, and I don't think I could get rid of it even if I was serious.

Autumn is not all fun and games. Some cleaning has to take place, though it isn't a big priority around here. I usually use the good old-fashioned method of weed-and-feed by pulling out weeds not in seed and just leaving them in place to compost down. I don't really care if it isn't perfect, but my ego and good sense haven't deserted me completely. I don't let piles of junk mount up. Slugs and other creatures would view that as a winter spa. I sweep paths and areas where there is stone or brick and leave most plants uncut except for anything hit by mildew — they are moved out pronto.

Cleaning up may be a little finicky, but it's also a lot of fun. It's a good time to learn more about plants past their prime. It's easier to decide whether they stay or should be sent to the trash heap. I can get pretty ruthless this time of year, mainly because I can feel the cold breath of winter just ahead. Out come the under-performers, the scraggly and the just plain boring. In go all those great sale plants. Sometimes we hang on to plants for far too long. I did this with yellow loosestrife, *Lysimachia punctata*. Not a terrible plant by any means; in fact, it's quite pretty, but it's invasive and the space it's likely to take up should be given to plants that are more important in a small garden. It's also one of those plants that will take over once it has escaped the garden into the wild.

Don't confuse this with purple loosestrife, *Lythrum salicaria*, a very destructive plant with no known enemies, that will overwhelm and destroy wetlands if it's let loose. It's a gorgeous plant but an alien that shouldn't be permitted in the garden and, if planted, should certainly never be allowed to go to seed. Even

Above left: In the background there's a mislabelled *Sambucus canadensis*. It was supposed to be the golden form, but is the ordinary European elder. It doesn't matter because the fruit is so rich and heavy, and watching flocks of birds come in to eat is part of the fun. The silky plumes in the foreground are from the grass, *Miscanthus sinensis* 'Sarabande', which has a subtle variegation on its leaves. Above right: The deep burgundy leaves of *Viburnum plicatum tomentosum* 'Shasta' stand out in stark contrast to another miscanthus, *M. s.* 'Morning Light', which will get to be a riot of color all by itself in burnished copper tones.

Above left: This is a great little boxwood called *Buxus sempervirens* 'Aureo-variegata'. It has a soft yellow edging and will very slowly get to be about 6 feet. Above right: Nearby, but a little further on is a pencil-slim juniper, *Juniperus virginiana* 'Blue Arrow', whose function is to pull the eye deeper into the garden during autumn and winter. It's pretty much drowned out by foliage the rest of the year. This is a neat plant and will get tall though stay slender. Evergreens should be placed carefully throughout the garden to give autumn and winter interest and to act as background plants and companions for important shrubs.

the sterile hybrids aren't as sterile as we once assumed. I tried getting this plant out of my garden by exposing the root system over the winter and pouring boiling water over it, and it still survived.

Scraping the ground clean is a big mistake in any garden, because leaves return most of the nutrients crucial to soil health. I used to love crawling around as a kid and watching autumn leaves fold up like little handkerchiefs and eventually disappear into the ground. What I didn't know then was that ambitious worms were pulling them into the soil to digest them and consequently fertilize the earth. I allow worms to do much of the work these days and let fallen leaves lie. They are usually gone by spring. If I have bagged leaves, I put them in an out of the way corner to be added slowly to the compost bin over the next year.

Fragile plants also get a covering of evergreen boughs. The really iffy plants (and I count new shrubs in that category) will get compost, the ordinary mulch and boughs in the hope that these will help them through the important first winter. Any tricky plants that have managed to get past the magic two or three years are treated normally. If they are lucky, they might eventually get mulched.

One end-of-season chore I adore is to stand around with a hose, dribbling water at the bases of plants and generally sniffing and gazing around the garden. This is one of those incomparable moments when you can smell the plants more intensely than at any other time of the year.

Another favorite autumn job is screening compost. I'll spend hours quietly rubbing this gorgeous stuff over a metal screen (listening to opera on headphones) and picking out the little red wigglers that do all the work of breaking down compost. They are thrown back into the bin, since they won't survive in ordinary garden soil. Mindless and totally relaxing.

This is also a good time to build up the compost. I've always layered kitchen scraps, leaves and garden wastes and keep it fairly moist. Once it dries out, the temperature will lower and decay will slow down measurably. When a hard frost hits, I have bags of compost, coco-fiber and manure all mixed together to spread around where mulch is needed the most, as deeply as I've got material for.

About 10 years ago, I started planting hundreds of bulbs every year. Just little bulbs so that they aren't a such a huge effort. But what a bonus they are: scillas, grape hyacinths, species tulips and narcissus. They don't take up much space, and they can be mushed together without any glaring errors in color coordination.

I've often been astonished, as I crawl around planting bulbs, by the number of slugs that abound at this time of year. If I haven't hand-picked them every day, this is when both the plants and I pay for it. Some of the paler hostas are gobbled right to the ground. One thing I usually do as a last-minute autumn job is to make a tea of wormwood, *Artemisia absinthium*, and pour it around hostas, hoping to bump off overwintering slugs that have gone underground.

Another absorbing chore is the combination of planting new bulbs and perennials, and dividing up old ones. I do this weeks before the frost, which usually hits at the end of October or early November. This is when I can see exactly what's wrong with things, where I've made the big mistakes. The soil is still a pleasure to work with, and both kinds of plants can get a good crack at putting down strong roots. Normally, we can count on rain to water new plants, but if not, I just let hoses dribble water in.

Planting bulbs with perennials means there will always be something to cover yellowing bulb foliage in the spring. I used to add bone meal in the bottom of bulb holes, but now I worry about mad cow disease — just whose ground-up bones are these, anyway? I pop bulbs in and give the usual top-dressing of compost. As soon as squirrels see an area of disturbed soil, they love to get their busy little hands involved. I spread blood meal around, imagining they hate the smell of death. But the best thing is to make new bulb plantings as inconspicuous as possible, so on go piles of leaves to disguise any signs of activity.

I don't like putting bulbs too close to shrubs, though I don't worry about planting them near perennials. Bulbs seem to know exactly which way is up and around if they happen to bump into anything. If I buy fall plants in bloom, it's nice to know what they'll look like, but I know it's necessary to bite the bullet and cut them back to the same height as the roots are deep. This allows them to concentrate on root growth and not bloom production. It's important to be especially gentle with plants that have been sitting around the nursery in pots all summer. They've probably been planted in soilless mix and will go into shock when they get a taste of the real stuff.

If the root systems look as if they are strangling, I cut into them, then put them into well-prepared beds. I leave them alone until after the ground has frozen and add mulch. If anything with nitrogen is added to the soil before this, it will encourage new growth that will be killed off by frost, depleting the plant's resources. It's singularly important for woody plants to have mature growth to be able to resist frigid temperatures.

Although this is an ideal time to plant trees and shrubs (and get roses into the ground before it freezes), wait until spring for evergreens. They transpire even more heavily than deciduous plants all winter long, and of course, it's impossible to water them. Frost and sunlight can be a killer combination, which is why you should plant early enough to avoid this mix. And be wary of any very still, moonlit night once the autumn shoulder has passed and nights are getting long. A cold air stream at ground level can bring damaging frost. Be careful of advection frosts (wind-borne from almost any direction) as well.

I always say my garden doesn't look like a disaster area in autumn, but to the alien eye, I'm sure it does. I've seen many gardens with leaves neatly mounded around trees and shrubs, with mulch laid out carefully, and wish I could be like that but I'm not. I'm a sloppy housekeeper too.

This is one of the three seating areas (including the deck) where I actually land on occasion. In the background is the dogwood, *Cornus alba* 'Siberica', which has fabulous red bark in winter. Next to it is the semi-evergreen leatherleaf viburnum, *Viburnum rhytidophyllum* 'Allegheny'. To me, the bench is ideally located but the obelisk, which has been moved from place to place, is not at all satisfying in this location. The scale is wrong: it is much too small and should be another couple of feet taller. The clematis will have to be cut back and a new obelisk will be installed. The garden always provides an opportunity for shopping.

stars of autumn

Angelica gigas
Asters
Autumn crocus
Boltonia
Cimicifuga/Actaea
Eupatoriums
Hamamelis
Itea virginica
Japanese maple
Mint shrub
Ornamental grasses

- When planting bulbs, cover them with a bit of soil, water well, wait for the water to drain, then fill the hole with the rest of the soil. Most bulbs will start growing roots within 24 hours of coming into contact with moist soil (just a trickle of water over the planted area won't do it).
- For balled-and-burlapped plants, make the hole the same depth as the root ball and five times the width, or at least a yard across.
- For container-grown plants, make the hole five times as wide as the container, and dig down deep enough that the top of the plant's root system will be just above the surface of the soil.
- Collect as many bags of leaves as you can. Grind them up if that's possible (borrow a mulching mower), then add a little soil or compost to the bag. Pile them up, then add them to the compost all winter long.
- Water evergreens deeply right until hard frost. Lack of water is one reason they turn brown in spring. Often, so-called winterkill is simply due to an oversight, not bad weather.
- Cut back perennials remaining in pots and store in a protected spot. I give them a good hit of water and, for added protection, surround them with the bubble plastic used to wrap furniture. If the plants survive, fine. If not, at least I know the pots won't crack up.
- Never give newly installed plants a dose of fertilizer close to the end of the season; it will encourage new growth that will likely be killed by frost.
- Don't prune trees in late summer; it will spur growth that won't have time to mature before winter.
- To combat slugs, mix 1 part ammonia with 10 parts water and douse the plants with it when they go into dormancy. Or make an infusion of *Artemisia absinthium* and pour it around the plants.

autumn tips

There is a certain kind of bliss in the brief moment between the old year and the new, when imagination becomes paramount.

winter

I can sit around for days with nothing else on my mind except what I'd like to grow next year, or what plants I'd like to move and where. Winter will never be my favorite time of the year, but I welcome it in a curious way. By the time November rolls around, I've pretty much done what I can in the garden. This is the start of a long season of dreaming and changing things around, if only in my head. The beauty of winter lies in its serenity. The garden may be exposed and at its most vulnerable, but it has more to reveal than at any other time of the year.

Time and the garden have always puzzled me. In spring, I'm convinced I will have time to do everything I want. Before I know it, winter is upon us and I haven't done half of what I had planned. Maybe it's because the planning always takes place during winter, when long days in the garden appear to stretch out luxuriously forever. I feel more like a little kid in winter than in any other season — all expectations and grandiose dreams. The fact that other events might interfere, that various desirable plants aren't available, that a certain tree or shrub or even humble perennial simply can't be taken out or moved doesn't occur in the depths of winter.

In winter, everything is possible. I know that the minute I turn my back on the garden, it gets larger in my head. Facing reality, however, is a serious part of gardening, and I always have to struggle with the knowledge that I have a small garden with plenty of limitations.

This is the season we spend more time looking at the garden than being in it. Therefore, you'd think we would concentrate on having magnificent winter gardens. Unfortunately, this seems to have eluded most people for whom putting the garden to bed means just that — out of sight and out of mind. I admire people whose gardens look handsome in winter. These are not places full of mummified plants shrouded in burlap. These are the gardens where just the right kind of furniture has been left out to accumulate snow and look sculptural, where there is shape and form even without surrounding foliage.

Now is the time I pore through the books, magazines and catalogues that I haven't had time to even open the rest of the year. I'm prone to lists and, sometimes, can even find them when the time is ripe. A notebook is always good, but which is the one with the current plant wish list? The serious place of reckoning is in my daily garden journal. I have been devoted to this since the mid-1980s, and it's one activity about which I'm really disciplined. I record what's happening in the garden and what the weather is like. I expect it to be my *aide-mémoire* well into old age.

Gardens aren't like paintings or buildings or bridges. They alter not only over great lengths of time but almost every day. Apart from the changes every day in every season, there is also a shift of light from hour to hour. It's hard to juggle this in your mind and to keep a firm grasp on what the garden is expected to accomplish, especially in the dead of winter. Everything looks so calm, and there is little to interfere with the eye. It's easy to dream up some grand design, but it requires an iron grip to keep everything in perspective.

This poignant sight always makes me elated that *Rosa* 'The Fairy' will hang right on into winter and, at the same time, a little sad that the season is truly finished. Winter seems long but it is usually so busy with plans, books and a year of unread magazines that it passes quickly and, in most cases, creatively.

I redesign as an annual exercise even though I love my garden as it is. But how tempting to rip everything out and start again.

To compensate for this foolishness, I usually work on pockets in different parts of the garden. It keeps my failures private. And by replacing all the plants in a modest area, though it will certainly influence the look of things nearby, it won't dictate changing absolutely everything else in the garden. I also think this is the best way to get some real style into any garden without losing continuity.

I started planting grasses and evergreens in a small space in Le Jardin des Refusés. This screamed for some kind of contrasting background to enhance their light, frothy quality. So I put in large deciduous shrubs such as viburnums, a magnolia and a katsura. The shrubs needed new surroundings. In this case, I planted ferns (there are such good ones now available), which meant that more woodland plants had to be found for the next area. And so it goes; one thing leads to another, usually quite logically if I do a little creative staring.

By contemplating my garden all that critical winter before I renovated the whole place, I found that it was the spaces I was looking into. My mind wasn't cluttered with the fact of plants, or plant color, or plant volume. There was just space in front me. By rearranging the spaces in a flat, two-dimensional way, I was able to impose some kind of order on this exceedingly dull area. I could also see the big task, and that was to deal with the garden's bowling-alley proportions.

This narrowness was restricting in the extreme. My little epiphany about the checkerboard was a revelation in more ways than one. The checkerboard gave definition to the interior space of the first section and made it look much larger. I also chose to ignore the rest of the garden so that I wasn't tackling more than I could cope with, thereby eliminating a great many problems that I had neither time nor money to solve.

I understood the need, almost immediately, for having a truly effective winter setting. It was all too apparent: there was no color here, no pleasing volumes to give the garden dimension, just a rag-tag bit of planting. Once the leaves had gone from the trees and that vital sense of being cosseted was lost, it needed something drastic. That meant more evergreens, more grasses, colored bark, dramatic shapes everywhere.

As usual in gardening, I picked up ideas all over the place. I used to call it creative stealing. Now I just think of it as creative. I knew designers who were really good at winter landscaping, and I tried to incorporate their best ideas into my own garden. I wish garden tours weren't just confined to the summer. This would be a really instructional time to look about.

For instance, one designer taught me about the importance of emphasizing shape. He employed three geometric forms to make his garden sing: the square, the circle and the pyramid, all of which work

A heavy snowfall can turn the garden from autumn dreck to winter magic overnight. Having enough plants around to hold the snow is important in any winter garden. Evergreen and semi-evergreen plants should be placed so that a pattern will emerge in winter. Colorful bark is just as important as leaves, as you can see from the coralbark maple at the far right. The rosy bark is echoed in the *Cornus siberica* to the rear.

Vines and shrubs decked out in winter finery include incredible berries. Birds choose these ones last. Opposite: Bittersweet, *Celastrus scandens*, is a rampant vine that's much too large for the garden but when I see the berries, I remember why I planted it. Above left: *Cotoneaster dielsianus* var. *major* is a splendid fountain-like vine with pale appleblossom-colored flowers in spring and tiny crimson berries in winter. Above right: The good old dogwood always has leaves that hang on and on.

naturally together. When you add one sculptural element, you need to counterbalance it with another while making sure that they are all in scale with the garden itself.

One of his basic premises was that color isn't of paramount value in creating form, and to use space instead. He would "plant" branches of cedar, birch and pussy willow to fill in empty gaps. The strong, square shapes of the existing raised borders were, he felt, too obvious. They needed to be complemented by other equally strong shapes. He chose the pyramid and the circle. He made pyramids by tying bamboo canes or long, slender branches of bright red dogwood together, clad them in chicken wire and then filled the interior with leaves. I've done a variation on this with bits and pieces of evergreen rescued at Christmastime and stuffed inside.

He made circles out of chicken wire using a hanging basket as the form, then once the basket was removed, jammed the wire shape full of leaves. Plunked into the large iron container, they took on the look of giant pomanders. Could there ever be a more esthetic way to recycle leaves? By spring, they are breaking down and can be dumped into the compost or spread around the garden as mulch. These simple, geometric shapes are almost like topiary. And because they have such wit to them, they could work in either a formal or an informal garden.

I start collecting material for the winter pots as late in autumn as I dare. I concoct humongous outdoor arrangements of twigs, evergreen cuttings, long stems of vines with berries on them, and dried alliums, which I always save, along with cuttings from ornamental grasses when their graceful plumes have developed. When backlit, they add their own bit of enchantment.

Lighting, of course, becomes paramount in winter. To get through these long, cold nights, we need all the help we can get. I become more grateful each year that I put light in the garden. Rather than looking into a void, I can see the shapes of plants, the obelisk covered in vines, major trees and shrubs and, best of all, the Japanese maple lit up dramatically. When the lights are covered with snow, they create even more interesting and mysterious shapes with their luster. The lights also help me see into the garden. I sometimes muck about in the cold, adjusting the direction of a light and then running back into the house to see where there are gaps to be filled next year.

Each year, I try to put in at least one new evergreen strictly for its winter interest. I think it's wise to introduce them slowly because they have such strong positive forms. They can be overwhelming, and too many make things look static. I try to look for something new, at least to me. One year, it was the low blue *Juniperus squamata* 'Blue Star' along with the steely tones of blue oat grass, *Helictotrichon sempervirens*. A good combination, but I got tired of it several years later and moved the plants. If winter is for anything, it's for changing your mind.

Any leaf that stays on during the winter gets my vote. It doesn't matter what kind they are, the patterns they make are so graphic I can spend a lot of time just staring at them. Above left is English ivy, *Hedera helix*, and above right, what's left of a clematis. The winter garden can be extremely animated if you look closely.

Above left: Snow perches precariously on the leaves of *Daphne* x *burkwoodii* 'Somerset', which will last through most of the winter. Above right: A yew, *Taxus* x *media* 'Hicksii', holds up bravely under a deep layer of snow. The painterly leaf (opposite) is from leatherleaf viburnum, *V. rhytidophyllum* 'Allegheny', and you can see the promise of next spring's blossoms in the little rounded bud.

I hate it when strangers come into my garden and say, "Oh, why don't you . . . ." But I do have one good friend who knows the poetry of this garden. When she speaks, I listen carefully. One year, she suggested putting a dark green yew behind the coralbark maple to give the red bark more intensity. So I did that. This also that meant I'd have to have another yew farther along on the other side to keep the eye moving incrementally deeper into the garden. Another year, she persuaded me to try a pencil-slim blue juniper beyond the coralbark maple and the yew. This is a plant that would never occur to me to want. But I followed her suggestion, and what a difference it makes. The eye is not only pulled into this small scene but beyond as well — to a wonderful grass in the same tone of blue called *Miscanthus sinensis* 'Prairie Sky'. This, naturally, will change what things look like in summer, and all those plants will then have to be reconsidered.

You can find good garden concepts in many different places. But most of us have ideas in our heads that we'll never, ever be able to accomplish. And most of us have horrible things to contend with, not the least being children, dogs, fire hydrants, neighboring buildings and trees. Taking all that into consideration, I still find it enlightening to listen to someone with a terrific eye make suggestions about the garden. I don't want a major critique (my ego's too involved with what I've already done). But you just never know when someone's going to come up with an idea for a new combination. And quite often an outsider can solve a problem far more easily than you can yourself because you get too close to it.

I've certainly picked up ideas from my decorator friends, one of which is to invest in one good piece of furniture and keep adding. Even if I couldn't afford much of it, I bought good garden furniture from the beginning. It started with four comfortable painted iron chairs, then a marble-topped table, then a mirror on the deck and some built-in statuary. They all hold the snow and cast beautiful shadows. It's very subtle, and the more you look at it, the more there is to appreciate. Because my garden is so enclosed, the part nearest the house has the feel of a courtyard to it. In this tranquil winter state with no one around and only ornamental grasses stirring close by, it maintains this sense perfectly.

I wish I could say the same about the front garden. The grass was removed to the berm years ago and, though I'd put in many plants, it never really satisfied me. Winter certainly brings out its imperfections. I look at it all day long from the window where I write. In my head, I've redesigned it a thousand times, and yet until a few years ago, nothing seemed able to make this an agreeable space. If I had my wishes, I'd replace the silver maple with a *Ginkgo biloba*. The latter has a reputation of growing very, very slowly. Well, not as slowly as you might think. I've watched one across the street reach imposing proportions in only a few years. It competes very nicely with the maples on the street, shows off in autumn with the most amazing gold color

Boxwood, *Buxus*, is a great plant for holding the snow without being destroyed by it. If snow gets too heavy, whack it off with a ski or anything long and flexible. To the left, *Artemisia* 'Lambrook Silver' is still looking good. Towards the fence, the blue juniper is starting to make its own statement. This is the view I have with my morning coffee which explains why it's rather more organized than the rest of the winter garden.

The look of winter is summed up in these photographs. They express the richness that persists all through the garden. Above left: Up close the hips of a *Rosa rugosa* seem enormous. They don't last the winter because the birds love them. Above right: Northern sea oats, *Chasmanthium latifolium*, is the best of all grasses, not just because of the amazing seed heads (fabulous for dried arrangements, by the way) but also for the fact that it can be flattened out by snow and spring back to life undamaged.

Above left: Oakleaf hydrangea, *H. quercifolia*, not only retains the remnants of its lovely lacecap flowers but also has exfoliating bark. The color is a deep cinnamon brown. This is one of those flowering shrubs that will bloom in its very first year. It requires almost no maintenance except to cut out dead bits in spring, and should be kept relatively moist. Above right: I'm fascinated by seed heads etched against a snowy background. This is another reason not to cut plants back to the ground in autumn or overtidy the garden.

and has a lovely vase shape in the winter. It's one of those miraculous trees that withstands pollution, which is what we've got a lot of in this city.

To improve the front garden's winter appearance, I began placing ornamental grasses judiciously about. They are a boon to any garden. They glisten in autumn with spikes of color and are strong enough to endure the fiercest winters by simply yielding to snow and then bouncing right back when it's brushed aside. Grasses also provide a rustling sound I find reassuring on clear, cold, blue winter days. The garden seems full of life.

There are now hundreds of grasses available in just about any color you can imagine. Here are just a few I've planted so that I can look at them all year in my front garden: *Miscanthus sinensis* 'Sarabande' and 'Sirene', *Pennisetum alopecuroides, Molinia caerulea* subsp. *arundinacea* 'Sky Racer' and *Chasmanthium latifolium*, and I'll add more as they find me. Because of the low light conditions, they took several years to really become established and the best is yet to come from these plants.

They stand out in stark relief against the surrounding shrubs. At first, it didn't occur to me to try and block out the street, since it's only 20 feet away. But the more densely I plant, the more this now seems a possibility. At least there is something to engage my eye other than the disintegrating old green Corvette one neighbor insists on keeping out front though he never drives it. Actually, I've grown to like this thing because it's just there. I envision planting the car with annuals and having vines growing over it to make a real horticultural statement. They can all compost down together.

Winter is also the time of year I'm really glad my kids have left home so they can't see just how crazed I can get. Occasionally, they say things such as "You never took that many pictures of us," though rather laconically. I would never have wanted them to see what was going on a few Januarys ago. We had a lot of snow and then it rained and then it froze, and all I could see was this skating rink in the back. I was in despair.

I got out with the big rubber boots, lugged buckets into the back and started hacking away at the ice, hauling huge chunks out to the front to fling into the road. When I realized I couldn't carry on alone, Mack, the strong young man from next door, was pressed into service. He never said a word, never rolled his eyes as we slaved on hour after hour. He was wearing his mum's rubber gloves over mitts and I was wearing huge rose-pruning gloves over mine. No amount of hot chocolate could compensate for how frigid our hands and feet became. It rained that night and froze again the next day, and all our work was for nought. I wish I could just stay put in winter and be still. But no. I've got to get frantic that the plants might not survive if I don't worry about them. Of course, the roots don't need any of my help, but my thoughts are with them. This is not anthropomorphism so much as the kind of knowledge that I think will help make me a better gardener. Winter was designed for research.

Even a shrub as small as this *Berberis thunbergii* 'Atropurpurea Nana' will keep snow in its place. The form is superb. A major consideration when picking out a woody plant is what it will look like in winter: will it hold the snow and become a sculptural shape or will it have some color in the bark?

Plants know when to close down for winter in ways that make survival possible. They slow down all activity. Leaves drop off so that the plant won't dry out as the roots take up less moisture. The water in plant cells changes so that it has a lower freezing point. This hardening-off occurs once temperatures sink between 0 and 5 degrees C (32–41 degrees F). When plants are cold-hardened, they can resist low temperatures without injury to branches and trunks. This is why it's important to introduce wintering-over container plants to the house on a gradual basis fairly early in the autumn. If they become cold-hardened, they will have no end of trouble adjusting to the desert conditions of a hot and dry house.

Each plant species has a temperature at which tissues will start to die. It could be as little as an hour's exposure or as much as six hours. And goodbye, plant. This narrow edge between injury and death is what we gardeners spend our time agonizing over. And it is one of the reasons I always have old sheets at the ready to throw over plants if there's a threat of early frost.

It's easy to forget that plants transpire moisture all the time, in all seasons, though more slowly in winter than in summer. This is true for deciduous as well as evergreen plants. Even twigs transpire, though it mainly happens through leaves. Being careful to water each woody plant deeply before hard frost is obviously very important.

Underground, there is another story to be told. It's the water in the soil that freezes, not the roots as I had first imagined. Roots have rigid cell walls and can withstand a lot of pressure. By the time the soil is frozen, of course, water isn't available to plants, and as they continue to transpire, they can become desiccated.

The temperature at which roots will be killed varies from species to species. For this reason, it's a good thing to pay attention to designated hardiness zones, especially in woody plants. Having this information will help you choose cold-hardy plants.

Hardiness zones are based on average minimum winter temperatures. The growing period in temperate climates is from last frost to first frost, or when the temperature reaches 5.5 degrees C (42 degrees F), which is when grass starts to grow. But the range of temperatures from winter to winter is inconsistent, as we've seen in recent warm winters in our area. Who knows what global warming will be bringing us, apart from confused and confusing weather patterns.

There are a lot of other variables at work as well, including the height above sea level, the prevailing winds, whether the plant is in a frost pocket or not and, especially, drainage. Apart from obtaining plants already acclimatized to your area, it's another reason to buy from local growers.

Naturally, this is great advice that I ignore. I buy plants from all over the place for the sheer joy of seeing how many different kinds of plants I can grow. Because any garden is filled with a variety of microclimates

I leave just about everything in the garden untouched so that there will be plenty of seed heads in winter, not only for foraging birds but also so I can see the shadows cast by the sun onto the pristine snow. This laissez-faire form of gardening will also protect perennials from the ravages of winter.

(those small areas that are more protected than elsewhere within the garden), I like to put these plants in different spots. If one doesn't do well in this spot, who knows, it might do well 5 feet away.

We all know that anyone with a thick, reliable blanket of snow has the best of all possible mulches. I have friends with a garden (filled with mostly herbaceous plants) that lies under several feet of snow all winter. They can grow more tender plants than I can. Under the snow, conditions are moderate and, more important, constant. Where I live, we deal with freeze–thaws all winter. The higher temperature lasts just long enough to thaw some of the moisture, then it freezes again. I expect a lot of winterkill in my garden but like to think of this as an opportunity to buy more plants. A good attitude is necessary to survive a northern winter.

When I look at my own garden, I can see all my mistakes in winter. One thing not balancing another; too many deciduous plants; not enough evergreen plants. I've never become impatient with this slow process of change, which is what gardening is all about. I don't like to hang a lot of heavy-duty philosophical baggage on the garden, but it has been my salvation in many ways. As I get older, I hear even older people talk about killing time. Well, I'm never killing time when I'm in my garden. I'm racing against time to get as much done with what time I've got left. This sobering thought keeps me quite sane.

People keep telling me that I could never leave this garden. I don't know, but I'm sure I could. I'm sure I have enough time to make another garden. I do know that I'll continue not to use chemicals, I won't stop moving plants around, I will keep on mixing native plants with interesting new hybrids even though this isn't politically correct. I won't ever stop loving plants for their amazing tenacity to hang in there and give us pleasure whether we want to notice it or not.

I'll continue to garden until my entire body gives out. As each part goes, I'll figure out a new way to garden without it. Already I'm thinking of more raised beds to cope with a body that might not be comfortable bending over so far, or with knees just a bit tight in the socket. I can see the day when troughs might dominate my garden so that I can work while seated.

I can also see the day when my garden will be only in my imagination, still giving me pleasure, still being a good companion. What the garden has provided in my life is a retrieval of that sense of infinite possibilities and the joy you have as a little kid: being able to relish the most basic physical play and allow your imagination to soar. I have the image of a child happily playing with a piece of string. That's me in the garden. It's something I know I will never lose.

The first hopeful signs of spring hit when the witch hazels start to bloom. This lovely one (above left) is *Hamamelis* x *intermedia* 'Diane', which has these red flowers in late winter, and crimson leaves all autumn. Above right: These little tulips stuck their heads above the ground and immediately got hit by the last snowfall. It only slowed them down and didn't stop them from turning into minor glories a few weeks later.

stars of winter

Blue juniper
Blue oat grass
Boxwood
Climbing hydrangea
Coralbark maple
Holly
Ivies
Mahonia aquifolium
Northern sea oats
Red-twig dogwood
Schizophragma hydrangeoides
Yew

salt-tolerant plants

Acer spp., Maple

Alnus, Alder

Betula pendula, European birch

Chaenomeles speciosa, Flowering quince

Cornus mas, Cornelian cherry

Elaeagnus angustifolia, Russian olive

Gleditsia triacanthos, Honey locust

Picea pungens, Colorado spruce

Pinus strobus, Eastern white pine

Rhus typhina, Staghorn sumac

numbers in bold indicate photograph references

map

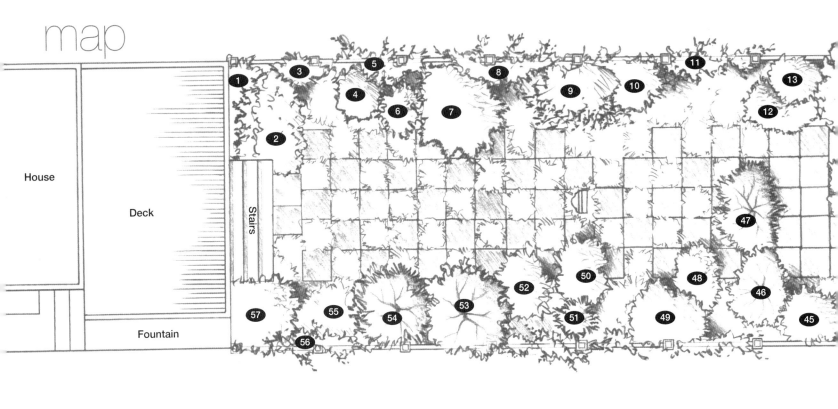

House

Deck

Stairs

Fountain

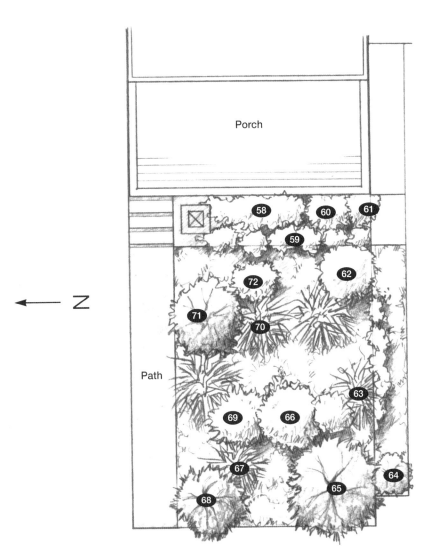

Porch

← N

Path

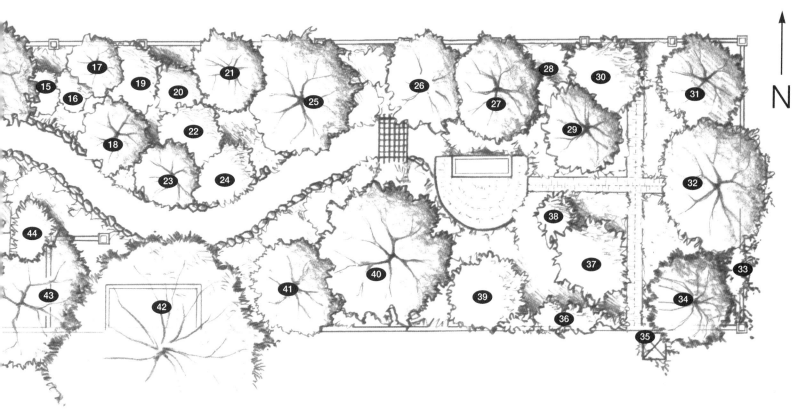

legend

1. Wisteria
2. *Boltonia asteroides*; *Lavatera* 'Barnsley'; *Geranium phaeum*
3. Bittersweet, *Celastrus scandens*
4. Red-leafed rose, *Rosa glauca* (syn. *R. rubrifolia*)
5. *Clematis* x *jackmanii*; *alpina* 'Ruby'; 'Blue Bird'; *terniflora*
6. Holly, *Ilex* x *meserveae* 'Blue Princess'
7. Butterfly bush, *Buddleia* 'Lochinch'
8. Japanese hydrangea vine, *Schizophragma hydrangeoides*
9. *Cotoneaster dielsianus* var. *major*
10. Oregon grape, *Mahonia aquifolium*
11. Porcelain vine, *Ampelopsis brevipedunculata* 'Elegans'
12. *Enkianthus campanulatus*
13. Oakleaf hydrangea, *Hydrangea quercifolia*
14. *Ginkgo biloba*
15. Witch hazel, *Hamamelis* x *intermedia* 'Diane'
16. *Acanthopanax sieboldianus*
17. Hicks yew, *Taxus* x *media* 'Hicksii'
18. Pagoda dogwood, *Cornus alternifolia*
19. *Viburnum* x *pragense*

20. Spike winterhazel, *Corylopsis spicata*
21. Silverleaf dogwood, *Cornus alba* 'Elegantissima'
22. *Viburnum* x *bodnantense* 'Dawn'
23. Star magnolia, *Magnolia stellata*
24. Variegated nannyberry, *Viburnum lentago* 'Variegatum'
25. Serviceberry, *Amelanchier canadensis*
26. Elder, *Sambucus canadensis*
27. Katsura, *Cercidiphyllum japonicum*
28. Father Hugo's rose, *Rosa hugonis*
29. *Magnolia* x 'Sundance'
30. *Viburnum plicatum tomentosum* 'Shasta'
31. Russian olive, *Elaeagnus angustifolia*
32. Kentucky coffee tree, *Gymnocladus dioicus*
33. Japanese hydrangea vine
34. Weeping silver pear, *Pyrus salicifolia* 'Pendula'
35. Obelisk and *Clematis viticella alba luxurians*; 'Elsa spath'; *texensis* 'Duchess of Albany'
36. Rugosa rose, *R. rugosa*
37. *Viburnum lanarth*
38. Shrub rose, *Rosa* 'The Fairy'
39. *Daphne* x *burkwoodii* 'Carole Mackie'

40. Redbud, *Cercis canadensis* 'Forest Pansy'
41. Cornelian cherry dogwood, *Cornus mas* 'Variegata'
42. Weeping willow, *Salix*
43. Dogwood, *Cornus alba* 'Siberica'
44. Leatherleaf viburnum, *viburnum rhytidophyllum* 'Allegheny'
45. Japanese kerria, *Kerria japonica* 'Picta'
46. Flowering dogwood, *Cornus Florida* 'Variegata'
47. Japanese maple, *acer palmatum* 'Dissectum Atropurpureum'
48. Dwarf fothergilla, *Fothergilla gardenii*
49. Climbing hydrangea, *Hydrangea petiolaris*
50. *Daphne* x *burkwoodii* 'Somerset'
51. Juniper, *Juniperus virginiana* 'Blue Arrow'
52. *Viburnum plicatum* 'Summer Snowflake'
53. Hicks yew, *Taxus* x *media* 'Hicksii'
54. Coralbark maple, *Acer palmatum* 'Sango-kaku'
55. Japanese hydrangea vine
56. *Clematis montana* 'Elizabeth'
57. Lilac, *Syringa vulgaris*

Front Garden:
58. Inkberry, *Ilex glabra* 'Compacta'
59. Coralbells, *Heuchera*, and new shrub hedge of *Heptacodium*; *Corylopsis*
60. Climbing hydrangea
61. Dwarf lilac, *Syringa velutina*
62. *Itea virginica* 'Henry's Garnet'
63. Bayberry, *Myrica pensylvanica*
64. Hicks yew, *Taxus* x *media* 'Hicksii'
65. Silver maple, *Acer saccharinum*
66. Dwarf lilac, *Syringa velutina*
67. Grass, *Molinia caerula* 'Sky Racer'
68. Arctic willow, *Salix purpurea* 'Nana'
69. *Viburnum plicatum* 'Summer Snowflake'
70. Grass, *Miscanthus sinensis* 'Sarabande'
71. Golden privet, *Ligustrum* 'Vicaryi'
72. *Viburnum farreri* 'Nanum' and an unknown ground covering pale pink rose

map **145**

acknowledgements

It seems pretentious to write a book about your own garden. This one has been seen so often on television and enough people have said, "I want to see more of your garden," that I've been led into temptation. Just about everything I write is based on what I do in this particular garden. As I've said before, it's my teacher, my guide and certainly my encyclopedia of plants. I try to grow everything to see if I can, and to see what really won't work in our climate. But I didn't get here alone.

I did all the work in the garden by myself in the early days, but now I get help. I'm not dumb. When I was really young, it seemed an impossible extravagance and I seldom hired anyone. Not so now that I'm older. I want the pleasure of the garden, not the pain. I still love to turn compost, dig holes, move things around, but I get bogged down lugging trees and shrubs about and ask others to do that.

A garden is always reinventing itself, and mine is no exception. All the following people, at some time or another, have contributed to this garden since we bought it in 1967. My son, Chris Harris, was the mainstay for many years until he got sideswiped by having children of his own. They haven't turned into gardeners yet — I live in hope. Ian Osgoode built most of the structures. David Cyana turned the potting bench into the best composter I've ever found. Curtis Dreiger installed the checkerboard. It was his idea to lift all the grass and make it into a berm, which really gave the garden the contours it has today. Gerry Cornwell designed the lighting. Ann Milovsoroff of the Royal Botanical Gardens is one of the few people whose every suggestion is acted upon. The late Murray Haigh was an inspiration, and I still mourn his loss. The fences were all constructed by different workmen whose names, alas, have been lost.

The people who've helped to make this garden so much fun: Cynthia and Tom McCarthy, Jacqueline Rodgers, Hester Gates, Charlotte Sykes and Anibal Fernandez. Keeping the garden in shape: Derrick Welsh of Authentic Tree Care, Lewis Arnold of Shady Lane and Victor Feodorov, who is always willing to help and give advice.

There are the nursery people who are incredible resources: John Valleau of Heritage Perennials, Tom Thomson of Humber Nurseries, Elke Kneichtel of Rainforest Gardens, Larry Davidson of Lost Horizons, Neil Turnbull of Hedgerow Organic Farm, the folks at The Plant Farm on Salt Spring Island, Dugald Cameron of Gardenimport, Annette McCoubrey of Cruickshank's, Carol Cowan of the Netherlands Flowerbulb Information Centre, and, especially, Val Ward of buds. They've given me wonderful plants to try and advice that works, and they are the kind of people who make gardening exciting because of their devotion.

There are the gardeners whose plants grace all parts of my garden and have been such an inspiration: Juliet Mannock, Susan Ryley, Pam Frost, Amy Stewart, Louise Kappus, Marion Jarvie, Anna Leggatt, Brian Bixley, Liz Knowles, Gwen Wilkes and Amanda McConnell. One of the great pleasures of my life has been writing a garden column for *The Globe and Mail*. I've done more than 200 columns since 1990, and some of this material appeared there first.

The people who worked with me on the book have been a total joy: Linda Read, who always found the missing fact, who read the first draft and made invaluable suggestions; Karen York, who not only gives me ideas for great plant combinations but also edited and botanically checked the book with her own special talent and sensitivity (the primary reference for the plant nomenclature in this book is the *A-Z Encyclopedia of Garden Plants*); Ian Montagnes, who lent me books; Andy Walsh, who wrote a great article on plant freezing, and Dr. W. Raymond Cummins, professor of botany, University of Toronto, who read the final material on the effects of cold on plants; Nicole Langlois and Iris Tupholme at HarperCollins, who are what you want in a publisher: cheerleaders who make great suggestions; and of course, Andreas Trauttmansdorff, who has been photographing the garden almost every two weeks for the past three years. Watching him troll through the garden in his own way opened up new images for me in my planting. I kept thinking, Will Andreas like this one? I also ignored him a lot of the time. He'd walk into the garden on occasion and find that something he'd photographed the week before was now gone. He added a whole new dimension to gardening, and it won't seem the same without his constant presence.

Marjorie Harris
Toronto, 1999

Marjorie and I have often spoken about our favorite movies while traveling together on editorial assignments, and it's in terms of movies that her garden might best be described. It is certainly not your typical Hollywood-type-of-movie garden. No. It is definitely more of a foreign-film variety of garden. None of the usual cardboard, overpaid American movie stars here. Rather, an array of often less recognizable but brilliant actors who almost certainly have a background in theater.

There is also not the usual beginning, middle and end. It's much less of a structure than it is a continual ebbing and flowing from week to week and season to season. It's the weather that supplies the continual plot twists. There are no car chases, no buildings being blown up, not even a good guy riding off into the sunset.

In their place, you find a series of delicately poetic little scenes, sometimes seemingly unrelated. Nonetheless, all are held together by an almost invisible theme. It's in the search for the meaning of that theme that you find yourself going back again and again, each time peeling back another of the many-textured layers. The closer you look, the more you are drawn in by all of the intricacies. In the end, whether or not you understand it all doesn't matter. It's the sense of feeling stimulated and rejuvenated that's most important.

I owe several people a profound thanks for their help in creating the images for this, my first involvement in an actual book. Above all, I thank Marjorie for asking me to be her partner in the project. When we first began working together, I knew nothing about gardening. It didn't seem to faze her at all. Now that we've worked together on various projects for almost four years, I still know nothing about gardening, and it still doesn't seem to bother her. Thank you, Marjorie.

Thank you to Bruce Chalmers and Agfa for transparency film with the most accurate color rendition available. Thanks to everybody at BGM Imaging for the excellent service, the endless use of the light table and all the envelopes. Thanks to HarperCollins for the opportunity to work with someone as great as Marjorie. And last, thank you to Alice Unger for taking a chance on me at a time when my portfolio was virtually void of anything to do with gardens.

Andreas Trauttmansdorff
Toronto, 1999